THE ESSENTIAL SCOTTISH FOOTBALL FAN

The Definitive Guide to Scottish Premier League, First, Second and Third Division Grounds

DUNCAN ADAMS

AP
AESCULUS PRESS LTD

www.aesculus-press.com

THE ESSENTIAL SCOTTISH FOOTBALL FAN

The Definitive Guide to Scottish Premier League, First, Second and Third Division Grounds

DUNCAN ADAMS

Cover by Acer Designs, Manchester
email: acerdesigns@aol.com

Published by

Aesculus Press Limited
PO Box 5276
Swadlincote
Derbyshire
DE11 9ZT

New edition

Typeset by Acer Designs

Printed and bound in Great Britain by
Ashford Colour Press Ltd., Gosport, Hampshire

1-904328-16-4

INTRODUCTION

Welcome to the first ever edition of the Essential Scottish Football Fan. Based on the acclaimed website www.scottishgroundguide.co.uk, the book covers every ground in the Scottish Premier League, the three Scottish Football Leagues and the national football venue, Hampden Park. Inside you will find a host of information useful to the travelling supporter. Not only are there practical details, such as directions to the grounds, but other information to make your day more enjoyable, such as pub recommendations. There are also of course a number of excellent photos of all the grounds themselves.

The book follows on from the success of the companion guide, The Essential Football Fan, which covers English and Welsh league grounds.

Having received a number of requests from fans asking for a Scottish version, it seemed a natural extension to do this. I have to say that I have thoroughly enjoyed my visits to the Scottish grounds and have been pleasantly surprised by the hospitality and helpfulness of Club staff and fans alike. It is has been a breath of fresh air.

Remember though that the Guide has been compiled based on not only my personal visits to the grounds, but the feedback of many supporters, who have visited them in recent seasons, giving an all around independent view. Without feedback, this book would not have been possible, so a big thank you to everyone who has contributed.

Although I have strived to make sure that every detail is up to date as it can be, things can change over the course of a season. For example a pub will close or another open, so please bear this in mind. I hope you find this guide useful and informative. But remember this is only a guide and should be treated as such. If you find that things have changed, feel that you can give better directions, or provide useful additional information, then please e-mail me at duncan@scottishgrounds.co.uk. Remember this guide is for football fans by football fans, so feel free to have your say. I'll strive, wherever possible, to include your comments in future editions.

ABOUT THE AUTHOR

My father, John Adams, who has now returned to live in his native Scotland, first took me to see a game when I was aged six in 1970 at Villa Park. The memories from that visit have always stayed with me. It was a cold winter's day, made a lot warmer by nearly 60,000 fans crammed into the ground for a league cup semi-final against Manchester United. The atmosphere was intense and I was soon hooked on attending games. But it was not Aston Villa but Birmingham City that became my love and I was soon a regular at St Andrews. As a teenager, I started to go to Birmingham away games and my fascination with different football grounds really began.

Since then, it's me craning my head to try seeing more of a ground, after glimpsing a floodlight pylon in the distance, from a car or train window. These stadiums are just so different from any other type of building you come across. Plus, when you add the fans, a football game, the atmosphere, then these places take on a magic all of their own. Having visited all 92 Premier and Football League grounds in England and Wales, the websites and books have given me further impetus to visit even more grounds than I originally had ever envisaged. I now have a fascination for the last surviving old grounds and stands, as well as to marvel at the new structures that seem to go up every year.

I hope you enjoy the book and that it will improve your away trips, as well as perhaps whetting the appetite to visit a ground that you hadn't thought about visiting before.

Duncan Adams
June 2004

Special Thanks
To Han van Eijden for his continual support and his mine of football knowledge over the years. To Ian Dewar, an exiled Nottingham Forest fan in Canada, for re-writing parts of the Guide so that it became immensely more readable. To Owen Pavey for providing a number of great photographs, as well as Matthew Day, Peter Llewellyn, Jean-François Foxhal & Peter Subach for their contributions. To Thomas Mapfumo of European Football Statistics for providing the average attendance information, please visit his website at www.european-football-statistics.co.uk. I am also indebted to Simon Inglis and his book 'The Football Grounds Of Great Britain' for some of the historical information contained within this Guide. And lastly to my wife Amanda, for her unquestioning support and patience in my ground visiting travels and putting this book together.

www.scottishgroundguide.co.uk

CONTENTS

SCOTTISH PREMIER LEAGUE

OTHER DIVISIONS

NATIONAL STADIUM

ABERDEEN

Ground Name: Pittodrie Stadium
Capacity: 22,199 (all-seated)
Address: Pittodrie Street, Aberdeen, AB24 5QH
Telephone No: 01224-650-400
Fax No: 01224-644-173
Ticket Office: 01224-631-903
Pitch Size: 110 x 72 yards
Club Nickname: The Dons
Home Kit Colours: Red & White
Official Website: www.afc.co.uk
Unofficial Websites:
Dandy Dons - www.dandydons.co.uk
Red Final Fanzine - www.redfinal.com
The Red Ultras - www.red-ultras.com
Dons In Europe - www.donsineurope.co.uk

WHAT'S THE GROUND LIKE?

At one end of the ground is the newest and largest stand, the impressive looking Richard Donald Stand, named after a former Club Chairman. It was opened in 1993 and replaced what was known as the Beach End. This is two-tiered with a row of executive boxes running across the middle. There is a particularly large lower tier, with a smaller upper tier and this stand tends to dwarf the others around it. The other end is a much smaller, older single-tiered stand called the Merkland Stand. On one side is the old Main Stand, originally built in 1925. As you would expect from an older stand, it has a fair few supporting pillars running along the front of it. Opposite is a large single-tiered cantilever stand, called the South Stand. The corner between this and the Merkland Stand is filled with seating, but this area is the only uncovered area of the ground.

FUTURE GROUND DEVELOPMENTS

After abandoning the proposal to build a new stadium at Bellefield, the Club are now talking to Aberdeen City Council about the possibility of building in partnership a new community stadium in the North Beach area of the city. The proposals at the moment are only that, but if they do make it off the drawing board then a state of the art stadium would be built, which would include a retractable roof, the first ever to be used at any league ground. Pittodrie would be sold off for residential re-development.

WHAT'S IT LIKE FOR VISITORS?

Away fans are housed on the one side of the South Stand. Up to 4,500 supporters can be accommodated in this part of the ground (although the normal allocation is around 2,500). Peter Llewellyn adds: 'There is normally an excellent atmosphere within Pittodrie, although it is sometimes lacking for the smaller games'. I think Pittodrie gets the vote as one of the coldest grounds in Britain. Even in spring the biting breeze off the North Sea, which is only a few hundred yards away from the perimeter of the ground, can go right through you. Outside, look out for the granite entrance to the Merkland Family Stand. Erected in 1928 they celebrate Aberdeen being known as the 'Granite City'.

WHERE TO DRINK

There are not that many pubs nearby, so consider drinking in the city centre before moving onto the ground. Scott McKenzie informs me: 'The nearest bar to the ground is the Broad Hill bar at the back of the Richard Donald Stand, but unfortunately this has a big sign up saying "home support only", although it hasn't always been that way. Next closest are the three golf clubs, all of whom operate a signing in/membership type thing, which some away fans do take advantage of and the atmosphere is invariably friendly. If travelling by coach, then all coaches are parked on the Beach boulevard, which is close to a bar called 'The Saltoun', popular with away fans. Otherwise there are plenty of bars to chose from in the city centre'.

GETTING THERE & WHERE TO PARK

The ground is located in the North part of the city (close to Old Aberdeen) and near to the coast line. It is close to the A956.

From The South:
Follow the A90 towards Aberdeen. Just south of Aberdeen join the A956. Keep on the A956 through Aberdeen and eventually you will come to Pittodrie over on your right. Turn right into Pittodrie Street for the ground.

From The North:
Follow the A956 into Aberdeen. You will reach Pittodrie over on your left. Turn left into Pittodrie Street for the ground.

From The West:
Follow the A96 into Aberdeen. At the large roundabout with the A978 turn left into Machar Drive (A978). Proceed along the A978 and then turn right onto the A956 (King Street). Pittodrie Street and the ground is the fifth turning on the left.

There is a large car park at the ground but this is for pass holders only. There is though a fair amount of street parking in side streets and on the Esplanade along the sea front, which is on the other side of the golf course.

By Train
Aberdeen train station is over two miles from the ground and is quite a walk (around 25-30 mins). Best to jump in a taxi to the ground. However if you want to brave the walk:

On leaving the station turn left and walk across the bridge and then turn right. This brings you into Union Street, where you should walk down until its end, where you will reach Castle Gate. Home supporters should bear left into King Street (A956) and continue down this street before turning right into Merkland Road for the ground. Away supporters should proceed through the Castle Gate and into Park Street. This street eventually becomes Golf Road and you will come to Pittodrie on your left. Thanks to Tom Widdows for providing the directions.

LOCAL RIVALS

Although not local, Glasgow Rangers.

ADMISSION PRICES

Like a lot of clubs, Aberdeen operate a category (A, B & C) pricing structure for match day tickets, whereby the most popular games cost more.

Home Fans:
Main Stand:
Adults: £28 (A), £25 (B), £22 (C).
Concessions: £20 (A), £18 (B), £15 (C).
Under 12s: £12 (A) £10 (B) £8 (C).
Richard Donald Stand:
Adults: £23 (A), £20 (B), £17 (C).
Concessions: £18 (A), £15 (B), £12 (C).
Under 12s: £11 (A), £9 (B), £7 (C).
South Stand:
Adults: £20 (A), £18 (B), £15 (C).
Concessions: £15 (A), £10 (B), £7 (C).
Under 12s: £8 (A), £6 (B), £4 (C).
Merkland Family Stand:
Adults: £18 (A), £15 (B), £12 (C).
Concessions: £10 (A), £8 (B), £5 (C).
Under 12s: £8 (A), £5 (B), £2 (C).
Away Fans:
South Stand:
Adults: £20 (A), £18 (B), £18 (C).
Concessions: £15 (A), £10 (B), £10 (C).

PROGRAMME & FANZINE

Official Programme: £2.50.
Ten Men Went To Mow (10MWTM): £1.

RECORD ATTENDANCE

45,061 v Heart Of Midlothian, Scottish Cup, March 3rd 1954.

AVERAGE ATTENDANCE

2003-2004: 10,389 (Premier League).

DID YOU KNOW?

In 1978 Pittodrie was the first football league ground in Britain to become all-seater.

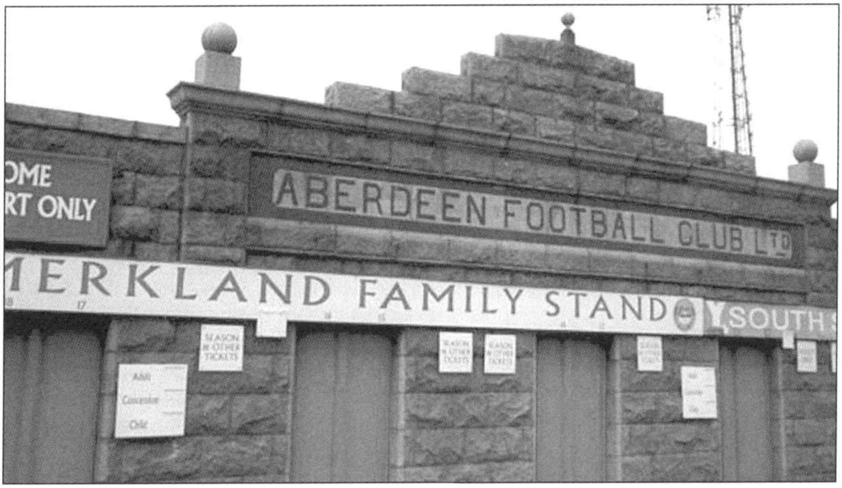

CELTIC

Ground Name: Celtic Park
Capacity: 60,832 (all-seated)
Address: 18 Kerrydale St, Glasgow G40 3RE
Telephone No: 0141-556-2611
Fax No: 0141-551-8106
Ticket Office: 0141-551-8653
Ticket Office Fax: 0141-551-4223
Stadium Tours: 0141 551 4308
Pitch Size: 105m x 68m
Club Nickname: The Bhoys
Home Kit Colours: Green & White Hoops
Official Website: www.celticfc.net
Unofficial Websites:
Jinky Soars - www.jinkysoars.co.uk
Celtic Paradise - www.celtic-paradise.co.uk
Bhoyzone - www.bhoyzone.net

WHAT'S THE GROUND LIKE?

Celtic Park (although known to many fans by the name of the Parkhead area in which it is situated) is simply a massive stadium that can be seen from miles around. Three-quarters of the ground have been redeveloped in recent years greatly improving the overall look. The ground is totally enclosed, with the three new sides being two-tiered. The lower tiers of these stands are huge and come up to roughly the same height as the older Main (South) Stand which is also two-tiered, just showing how large they are. The upper tiers of the new North Stand do have a few supporting pillars, which may obstruct your view (the Club do, however, issue reduced price tickets for those seats affected). The Main Stand is unusual as it has a large roof, most of which is translucent, which makes it look quite striking. The translucency helps keep the pitch in good condition. A television gantry is also suspended from beneath its roof. However, with the Main Stand being far smaller than the other sides, the ground looks a little imbalanced. Still if this was to be redeveloped at some point in the future then I'm sure Celtic Park would be in the running for the best club ground in Britain. I understand, though, that this may be sometime off as the Main Stand is a listed building. There are also two large video screens suspended from beneath the roof at either end of the ground. The quality of the image shown on these screens is superb. Another unusual aspect of the ground is that it has a number of seats that can be heated in cold weather.

David Murphy adds: 'A poll undertaken by BBC Radio 5 Live in 2003, resulted in Celtic Park being voted as the 'most atmospheric sports venue' (note, not just football) in the UK'.

WHAT'S IT LIKE FOR VISITORS?

Away fans are housed in the lower corner of the Lisbon Lions Stand at one end of the ground. The views of the playing action and the facilities provided within this stand are excellent. There are also betting facilities available within the ground. The atmosphere within Celtic Park is normally superb and it is a great stadium to watch football. As most games are normally sold out, make sure that you have a match ticket before you decide to travel.

WHERE TO DRINK

As would be expected, most bars around the Parkhead area are partisan and particularly busy. It is probably best to drink in the city centre beforehand. However most of these bars will not serve fans wearing football colours.

GETTING THERE & WHERE TO PARK

The ground is on the East side of Glasgow on the A74 (London Road).

From The South:
Stay on the M74 until its end and then continue into Glasgow on the A74. You will come to the ground after about a mile and a half on your right.

From The North:
M80 then onto the A80 towards Glasgow and then join the M73 South. At the end of the M73 join the M74 northbound. Stay on the M74 until its end and then continue into Glasgow on the A74. You will come to the ground after about a mile and a half on your right.

From The East:
Leave the M8 at Junction 8 and follow the M73 South. At the end of the M73 join the M74 northbound. Stay on the M74 until its end and then continue into Glasgow on the A74. You will come to the ground after about a mile and a half on your right. There is plenty of street parking to be had, especially in the side streets off the London Road going down towards the A74. Don't be surprised though, as you get out of your car that some kid appears uttering the words 'mind yer car mister?'

By Train
Glasgow Central and Queens Street railway stations are around a 30 minute walk away from the ground. Probably best to jump in a taxi (about £5). Otherwise if you arrive at Glasgow Central you can take a local train to Dalmarnock station which is about a 10 minute walk away from the ground. As you come out of the station entrance, turn right and proceed to the end of the road. Turn right into Dalmarnock Road and cross this road to the other side. Continue under the bridge and up to the traffic lights where you turn left into Springfield Road. Just carry straight on along this road and you will soon see the stadium appear in the distance ahead of you, over to your left.

LOCAL RIVALS

Rangers.

ADMISSION PRICES

The Club operate a category system of games, so that the most popular games are priced more than others.

Adults: £24-£33. Concessions: £14-£25.

In addition, there are a number of 'restricted view' tickets available, which on an adult ticket are £3 cheaper than the price quoted above.

PROGRAMME & FANZINES

Official Programme: £2.
More Than 90 Minutes Fanzine: £2.
Not The View Fanzine: £1.50.

RECORD ATTENDANCE

92,000 v Glasgow Rangers, 1938.

AVERAGE ATTENDANCE

2003-2004: 58,181 (Premier League).

STADIUM TOURS

The Club offer regular tours of the stadium, which cost £8.50 for adults and £5.50 for children. Tours should be booked in advance by calling 0141 551 4308.

DID YOU KNOW?

With a capacity of 60,832, Celtic Park is the largest football league ground in Scotland and the second largest in Britain.

DUNDEE

Ground Name: Dens Park
Capacity: 12,085 (all-seated)
Address: Sandeman St, Dundee DD3 7JY
Telephone No: 01382-889-966
Fax No: 01382-832-284
Pitch Size: 101m x 66m
Club Nickname: Dark Blues
Home Kit Colours: Dark Blue, Red & White

Official Website:
www.dundeefc.co.uk

Unofficial Websites:
Dee-licious - http://dfcdelicious.homestead.com/GGmain.html
Boab's Dundee Site - http://members.tripod.co.uk/BoabL/index-3.html
Glasgow Dees - www.glasgowdees.tk

WHAT'S THE GROUND LIKE?

The overall look of the ground has greatly improved with the redevelopment of both ends. The Bobby Cox and Bob Shankly Stands are similar looking, both being single-tiered and roughly of the same height. Both sides are quite old looking stands. The Main (North) Stand is a covered seated stand, unusual in that it is oval in shape, meaning that those sitting on the halfway line are furthest away from the playing action. In fact at one time the whole ground was oval. It also has only a small amount of seats in the lower portion of the stand, with the bulk of the seating in the upper part. On the other side is a more conventional single-tiered stand that only runs for about two-thirds of the length of the pitch. Both these stands have many supporting pillars that may hinder your view.

FUTURE GROUND DEVELOPMENTS

In order to comply with Scottish Premier League (SPL) rules, that take effect for the new 2004/05 season, the Club are installing under soil heating this summer. This has come as a relief to supporters as the Club faced the prospect of ground sharing with near neighbours Dundee United or even going out of business all together.

WHAT'S IT LIKE FOR VISITORS?

Away fans are housed in the Bob Shankly Stand at one end of the ground, where up to 3,000 supporters can be accommodated. Then if required, a further 1,000 seats can be allocated in the Main (North) Stand towards the Bob Shankly End. The facilities within the Bob Shankly Stand are quite good and the view of the playing action is excellent. The great thing about this stand is that even a relatively small number of away fans can really generate some noise. George Hobb, a visiting Hearts supporter, adds: 'Normally a relaxed and friendly day out and the atmosphere within the ground can be quite good'.

WHERE TO DRINK

The Centenary bar near to the ground welcomes both home and away supporters. The bar has two rooms within it, one of which is used for home fans and one for away supporters. George Hobb recommends: 'The Clep bar on Clepington Road. Great pies, friendly bar staff and very reasonable prices. It is only a five minute walk from the ground'.

GETTING THERE & WHERE TO PARK

Follow the A90 through Dundee. Leave the A90 at the junction with the B960 (signposted 'Football Traffic'/Dundee), and turn right onto Clepington Road (B960). Continue along Clepington Road for one mile where you will reach a roundabout. Go straight across the roundabout and after a short distance you should be able to see some floodlights over beyond the houses on your right. Take the second right into Arklay Street and then right into Tannadice Steet. Dens Park is up at the

end of this street on the left. There is an official car park behind the Bob Shankly Stand which costs £2 per car, otherwise street parking.

By Train

Dundee train station is more than two miles away from the ground and is quite a walk as well (25-30mins). Best to jump in a taxi.

LOCAL RIVALS

Dundee United.

ADMISSION PRICES

Like a number of Clubs, Dundee operate a category system (A & B), whereby the more popular games (Rangers, Celtic and Dundee United) cost more to watch than others. Prices are below with category B prices shown in brackets.

Home Fans:
Main (North) Stand: Adults £20 (£17).
Concession £12 (£10).
Family Area - Adults £14 (£12).
Concessions £10 (£8). Under 12s £8 (£4).
Other areas - Adults £16 (£14).

Away Fans:
Adults: £20 (£17). Concessions: £12. (£10).

PROGRAMME

Official Programme: £2.

RECORD ATTENDANCE

43,024 v Glasgow Rangers, Scottish Cup, February 1953.

AVERAGE ATTENDANCE

2003-2004: 7,090 (Premier League).

DID YOU KNOW?

The Bob Shankly Stand is named after a former manager of Dundee and brother of the legendary Bill Shankly, of Liverpool fame.

DUNDEE UNITED

Ground Name: Tannadice Park
Capacity: 14,209 (all-seated)
Address: Tannadice St, Dundee DD3 7JW
Telephone No: 01382-833-166
Fax No: 01382-889-398
Pitch Size: 110 x 72 yards
Club Nickname: The Terrors or The Arabs
Home Kit Colours: Tangerine & Black
Official Website:
www.dundeeunitedfc.co.uk
Unofficial Website:
Dundee United Mad (Footy Mad Network)
www.dundeeunited-mad.co.uk

WHAT'S THE GROUND LIKE?

The ground was improved in the 1990s with the construction of two new stands and an extension to the existing Main Stand. One of these is the impressive two-tiered George Fox Stand, running along one side of the pitch. This stand has a large lower tier and a smaller top tier. It opened in 1992 and was named after a former Chairman of the Club. On the other side is the Main (South) Stand, which was renamed the Jerry Kerr Stand in 2003, after a former player and manager. As Aidan Hegarty informs me: 'The original Main Stand was opened in 1962 and holds a place in the history of Scottish football grounds in being the first in Scotland to be constructed with a cantilever roof to provide column free viewing'. It is also unusual in that the stand is slightly 'L'-shaped, just extending around the South East corner of the stadium. Niall Wallace adds: 'It was intended at the time that the whole ground would be rebuilt in a similar manner to the Main Stand, but due to lack of finance it never happened. It is worth noting though that the Club was the first ever to have a glass fronted lounge in the Main Stand for the benefit of sponsors. This was opened in 1971 and overlooked the pitch, something that is now a common sight in grounds across the country today'.

The Main Stand was extended in 1997

so that it now runs the full length of the pitch. The extension replaced what was known as the 'Fair Play Enclosure', so named as it was funded from an award made to the Club from UEFA in 1987. The stand is two-tiered and has a strip of perspex running across the back of it, just below the roof, to allow more light to reach the pitch. The relatively new extension to the stand can be identified as it has an unusual roof jutting out towards the pitch. At one end of the ground is the West Stand (known affectionately as 'The Shed'), a former terrace with seating now fitted. Parts of the original terrace that are no longer used for spectators can be seen on either side of it. There are a couple of supporting pillars in this stand that could hinder your view of the pitch. Opposite is the covered two-tiered East Stand, opened in 1994.

FUTURE GROUND DEVELOPMENTS

From time to time it is suggested that a new stadium should be built in Dundee that would be shared by both Dundee Clubs. Whether this idea ever transpires remains to be seen.

WHAT'S IT LIKE FOR VISITORS?

Away fans are normally housed on one side of the Jerry Kerr (Main) Stand at one side of the pitch, where around 1,000 supporters can be accommodated. For old firm games and local derbies, then the whole of this stand plus the West Stand can also be given to the away support, increasing the allocation to around 5,400. George Hobb, a visiting Hearts supporter adds: 'The ground can sometimes lack a little atmosphere. Plus try to avoid arriving at the ground early, so that you get to miss that awful club mascot!'

WHERE TO DRINK

The Centenary bar near to the ground welcomes both home and away

supporters. The bar has two rooms within it, one of which is used for home fans and one for away supporters. George Hobb recommends The Clep Bar on Clepington Road. Great pies, friendly bar staff and very reasonable prices. It is only five minutes walk from the ground.

GETTING THERE & WHERE TO PARK

From The South:
Follow the A90 through Dundee. Leave the A90 at the junction with the B960 (sign posted 'Football Traffic'/Dundee), and turn right onto Clepington Road (B960). Continue along Clepington Road for one mile where you will reach a roundabout. Go straight across the roundabout and after a short distance you should be able to see some floodlights over beyond the houses on your right. Take the second right into Arklay Street and then right into Tannadice Steet for the ground. Street parking.

From The North:
Follow the A90 through Dundee. Leave the A90 at the junction with the B960 (sign posted 'Football Traffic'/Dundee), and turn left onto Clepington Road (B960). Then follow the directions as above.

By Train
Dundee train station is over two miles away from the ground and is quite a walk (30mins). Best to jump in a taxi.

LOCAL RIVALS

Dundee.

ADMISSION PRICES

Like a number of Clubs, Dundee United operate a category system (A & B), whereby the more popular games (Rangers, Celtic and Dundee) cost more to watch than others. Prices are below with category B prices shown in brackets.

Home Supporters:
Adults: £18-£20 (£16-£18). Concessions: £10-£11 (£9-£10). Children under 12 can purchase lower tier tickets for £4.

Away Supporters:
Jerry Kerr Stand (Upper Tier): Adults £20 (£18). Concessions £11 (£10).
Jerry Kerr Stand (Lower Tier): Adults £18 (£16). Concessions £10 (£9).

Concessions apply to under 18s and over 60s.

PROGRAMME

Official Programme: £2.

RECORD ATTENDANCE

28,000 v Barcelona, 1966,
Inter Cities Fairs Cup Competition.

AVERAGE ATTENDANCE

2003-2004: 7,722 (Premier League).

DID YOU KNOW?

That the grounds of Dundee United and their rivals Dundee, are literally only a few hundred yards apart on the same road. I believe that these two grounds are the closest together of any in Britain.

DUNFERMLINE ATHLETIC

Ground Name: East End Park
Capacity: 11,998 (all-seated)
Address: Halbeath Rd, Dunfermline, Fife KY12 7RB
Telephone No: 01383-724-295
Fax No: 01383-723-468
Ticket Office No: 0870-300-1201
Ticket Office Fax: 01383-626-452
Pitch Size: 115 x 71 Yards
Club Nickname: The Pars
Home Kit Colours: White With Black Stripes
Official Website: www.dafc.co.uk
Unofficial Website:
DAFC.NET - www.dafc.net

WHAT'S THE GROUND LIKE?

The overall look of the ground has greatly improved with the redevelopment of both ends of the ground. The Norrie McCathie and East Stands at each end of the ground are very similar in design and were opened in 1998. Both are covered single-tiered stands that are quite steep in appearance. On one side of the ground is the two-tiered South (Main) Stand, which is a classic looking football stand built in the early 1960s and is of a good size. On the other side is the smaller North Stand, which is single-tiered and partly covered (to the rear).
The Club accepted a grant from UEFA to replace their grass surface with a new experimental artificial pitch, which was installed for the 2003/04 season. Reaction to the new pitch has been mixed, especially when visiting sides lose on it!

WHAT'S IT LIKE FOR VISITORS?

Away fans are normally housed in the East Stand at one end of the ground, where just

over 3,000 fans can be accommodated. The facilities in this stand are good and the view of the playing action excellent. If demand requires it, then parts of the North and South (Main) Stand can also be allocated for a total of 6,783, which is the allocation for Old Firm games. Other visitors get a maximum of 4,400 seats. There is normally a good atmosphere generated within the ground.
One point of interest is that the winner of the half-time lottery is presented with the relevant amount of cash on the pitch. Let's just hope that they don't get mugged on the way home!

WHERE TO DRINK

Jim Francis recommends the Elizabethan for away supporters. Otherwise the ground is around 10-15 minutes walk away from the town centre where there are plenty of pubs to be found.

GETTING THERE & WHERE TO PARK

From The North and The South:
Leave the M90 at Junction 3. Take the A907 towards Dunfermline. Just keep going straight on this road and you will eventually come to the ground on your right.
From The West:
From the A985 take the A994 towards Dunfermline. Keep straight on this road into Dunfermline and you will come to the ground on your left.
Parking:
There is an official car park at the ground (£1) behind the East Stand. Otherwise street parking.
By Train
There are two stations that are each about 15 minutes walk away from the ground or about £4 in a taxi. These are Dunfermline Queen Margaret and Dunfermline Town. Both are served by trains from Edinburgh and the latter, as the name suggests, is closer to the town centre.

LOCAL RIVALS

Raith Rovers, Falkirk, Rangers and Celtic.

ADMISSION PRICES

Like a number of other clubs, admission prices are varied, dependant on the

category of opposition. The categories are 1, Old Firm Games, and 2, Other Games.

Home Fans:
Main Stand:
Adults: £20 (Old Firm), £17 (Other).
Concessions: £14 (Old Firm), £12 (Other).
Under 12s: £11 (Old Firm), £9 (Other).
Other Areas:
Adults: £18 (Old Firm), £15 (Other).
Concessions: £12 (Old Firm), £10 (Other).
Under 12s: £9 (Old Firm), £7 (Other).
Away Fans:
Adults: £20 (Old Firm), £18 (Other).
Concessions: £11 (Old Firm), £11 (Other).
Under 12s £11 (Old Firm), £11 (other).
Concessions apply to OAPs and under 18s. Unemployed and students can also purchase tickets up to two hours prior to kick off for £10. This offer applies to home supporters only.

PROGRAMME

Official Programme: £2:50.

RECORD ATTENDANCE

27,816 v Celtic, 1968.

AVERAGE ATTENDANCE

2003-2004: 6,236 (Premier League).

DID YOU KNOW?

One theory as to why the Club is nicknamed the Pars is that at one time the team played so badly they were labelled as a bunch of paralytics, which was later shortened to Pars.

HEART OF MIDLOTHIAN

Ground Name: Tynecastle Stadium
Capacity: 18,008 (all-seated)
Address: Gorgie Rd,
Edinburgh
EH11 2NL
Telephone No: 0131-200-7200
Fax No: 0131-200-7222
Ticket Office: 0131-200-7201
Pitch Size: 107 x 74 yards
Club Nickname: Hearts or Jam Tarts
Home Kit Colours: Maroon & White
Official Website: www.heartsfc.co.uk
Unofficial Websites:
International Hearts - www.heartsfc.com
JamboFever - www.jambofever.co.uk
London Hearts - www.londonhearts.com

WHAT'S THE GROUND LIKE?

The ground has improved greatly with the redevelopment of three sides of the stadium during the 1990s. The Roseburn, Gorgie and Wheatfield Stands are all good sized single-tiered stands that are similar in design and height. Only the Main Stand on one side of the pitch remains of the 'old' Tynecastle. Originally completed just after the First World War, it looks somewhat out of place amongst its shiny new neighbours. It is two-tiered, smaller than the other stands and has a fair few supporting pillars. There is a model of an owl perched on top of this stand to help deter the presence of other birds to the ground.

FUTURE GROUND DEVELOPMENTS

After agreeing with the Scottish Rugby Union and getting permission from the Scottish Premier League to move into nearby Murrayfield Stadium, the Club have since announced that they will continue to play at Tynecastle for the 2004/05 season. If the Club's finances do not improve though, then there is still an option to sell Tynecastle and move into the home of Scottish Rugby, but this is regarded upon as a last resort as it would be unpopular with the majority of Hearts fans.

WHAT'S IT LIKE FOR VISITORS?

Away fans are housed in the Roseburn Stand at one end of the ground, where up to 3,676 supporters can be accommodated. Clubs with a small following may find that a smaller portion of this stand is allocated. The steep slope ensures a good view of the pitch and the facilities on offer are good. Apart from the Old Firm games and local derbies against Hibs, the atmosphere can be lacking.

WHERE TO DRINK

George Hobb informs me: 'The Station Bar in Gorgie Road to the west of the stadium always has a warm welcome for away fans. Ryries and The Haymarket are good pubs and are within a 10 minute walk from the ground'.

He adds: 'Any neutral visitors should of course visit the legendary Athletic Arms, which is my favourite pub near the ground. The pub, nicknamed 'Diggers' as it overlooks a graveyard, serves great beer and has great service. In fact, it is not unusual to see fans just ordering with their fingers, as when you just indicate, two, three, four, the barman knows that you just want their excellent ale.
Other notable bars include the Tynecastle Arms, which is only a corner kick away from the ground and among the memorabilia on display is the Jersey worn by Super Wayne Foster when he scored the winning goal against Hibs in a cup tie a few years ago. For some more football memorabilia, John Robertson's bar is also worth a visit. Both these bars are located in Gorgie Road and get very busy on match days, so get there early'.

GETTING THERE & WHERE TO PARK

Follow the M8 towards Edinburgh. At the

end of the M8 take the A720 (Edinburgh bypass) southwards towards Dalkeith. Leave the A720 at the junction with the A71 and follow the A71 into Edinburgh. You will eventually reach the ground on your right. Street parking.

By Train

The nearest train station is Edinburgh Haymarket, which is a around a 15 minute walk from the ground. You can see the ground as you come into the station. On leaving the station, turn right at the Ryries pub, into Dalry Road which then runs into Gorgie Road. About one mile on and the ground is visible from the first major road junction/set of traffic lights.

LOCAL RIVALS

Hibernian, Rangers and Celtic.

ADMISSION PRICES

The Club operate a category system for matches so that admission prices are varied dependant on which club is being played:

Category A - Celtic, Rangers and Hibernian:

Wheatfield Stand:
Adults: £20. Concessions: £10 (Block A only). Gorgie Stand: Adults: £20. Concessions: £10.

Roseburn Stand:
Adults: £20. Concessions: £10.

Main Stand:
Adults: £18. Concessions: £10 (Blocks N and T only).

Category B - Other Clubs:

Wheatfield Stand:
Adults: £18. Concessions: £10 (Block A only).

Gorgie Stand:
Adults: £18. Concessions £10.

Roseburn Stand:
Adults: £18. Concessions £10.

Main Stand: Adults: £16. Concessions £10 (Blocks N and T only).

PROGRAMME & FANZINES

Official Programme: £2.
No Idle Talk Fanzine: £1.
ATB (Always the Bridesmaid) Fanzine: £1.

RECORD ATTENDANCE

53,396 v Glasgow Rangers, February 13th 1932,
Scottish Cup 3rd Round.

AVERAGE ATTENDANCE

2003-2004: 11,947 (Premier League).

DID YOU KNOW?

That the Club got its name from a local dance hall frequented by the founders of the Club.

HIBERNIAN

Ground Name: Easter Road
Capacity: 17,500 (all-seated)
Address: 12 Albion Place,
Edinburgh EH7 5QG
Telephone No: 0131-661-2159
Fax No: 0131-659-6488
Ticket Office: 0131-661-1875
Pitch Size: 112 x 74 yards
Club Nickname: The Hibees
Home Kit Colours: Green & White
Official Website: www.hibs.org.uk
Unofficial Websites:
Mass Hibsteria -
www.masshibsteria.com/home/index.php
Hibs Net (Rivals Network) -
www.hibsforum.co.uk

WHAT'S THE GROUND LIKE?

The ground has improved dramatically with three new stands being built at Easter Road over recent years. The latest addition is the new West Stand which was opened at the beginning of the 2001-2002 season. This is a particularly impressive two-tiered stand, which is now the largest stand at the ground. Its upper tier is much steeper than the lower, with a gap between housing corporate hospitality facilities. This stand is located at one side of the pitch, is unusual in having a large perspex strip in the upper tier, just below the roof, that allows more light into the ground. Both ends are relatively new and virtually identical to one another. Each is two-tiered and look unusual as a small corner of the top tier slopes away at an angle rather than being the normal rectangular shape. The East Stand at one side of the pitch is a former terrace that has now been made all-seated. This is the last of the older stands to remain and has a fair few supporting pillars. It also has a number of floodlight pylons protruding from its roof.

WHAT'S IT LIKE FOR VISITORS?

Away fans are normally housed in the lower tier of the South Stand at one end. However, if demand requires it, then the whole of the South Stand can be given to away supporters. Usually a good day out that is both enjoyable and hassle free.

Peter Llewellyn adds: 'On my last visit in May I was reminded of how near Easter Road is to the sea. It was a hot day when I set out and most fans were wearing just a shirt. A sea mist came down during the first half and obscured the top of Arthur's Seat which can be seen clearly in one of the corners. By the second half mists were swirling round the ground and Arthur's Seat had disappeared. The temperature went from about 25C to 6 or 7C and it was freezing. I didn't get completely warm until stopping for a bite to eat at Biggar on the way home!'

WHERE TO DRINK

Jim Adie, tells me: 'There are numerous pubs on Easter Road itself most of which are pretty friendly for away fans other than Aberdeen. The 'Four in Hand' and 'Middletons' are particularly recommended'. Ian McKenzie adds: 'Away fans (apart from the local rival clubs) should also be okay in the 'Cabbage N Ribs', also on Easter Road'.

GETTING THERE & WHERE TO PARK

Not the easiest of grounds to find as it is located in the North-East part of Edinburgh, on the other side of the City Centre where most people approach the city from the M8.

From The M8:

At the end of the M8, follow signs for the City Centre. Upon reaching the City

Centre follow signs for Leith (A900). At the B1350 junction, turn right onto London Road (B1350). It is then the fourth left at the crossroads, onto Easter Road, and then the fourth right into Albion Road for the ground.

From The South: (and avoiding the City Centre)

Follow the A1 into Edinburgh. Turn right onto the B1350 London Road and then right at the crossroads into Easter Road. Take the fourth right into Albion Road for the ground.

By Train

The ground is around a 20 minute walk from Edinburgh Waverley station. Exit the station via the Waverley Steps onto Prince's Street. Cross the road and head for Leith Walk which is about 200 yards diagonally opposite from the exit to the station. Go straight down Leith Walk for about a quarter-mile and turn right along London Road. Walk a further half-mile to the top of Easter Road on your left. The stadium is about 300 yards down Easter Road on your right-hand side. Thanks to Jim Adie for providing the train station information.

LOCAL RIVALS

Hearts.

ADMISSION PRICES

Admission prices vary in accordance with the category of the match. Category A prices are shown here with category B prices in brackets.

Home Fans:

West Stand Centre: Adults: £25 (£22). Concessions £10 (£10).
West Stand Upper Wings: Adults: £22 (£19). Concessions £10 (£10).
West Stand Lower Centre: Adults: £25 (£22). Concessions £10 (£10).
West Stand Lower Wings: Adults: £22 (£19). Concessions £10 (£10).
East Stand: Adults: £20 (£17). Concessions: £10 (£10).
Famous Five Stand Upper: Adults: £24 (£20). Concessions £10 (£10).
Famous Five Stand Lower: Adults: £22 (£19). Concessions £10 (£10).
South Stand Upper: Adults £24: (£20). Concessions: £10 (£10).

Away Fans:

South Stand Lower: Adults: £24 (£20). Concessions £10 (£10).

PROGRAMME & FANZINES

Official Programme: £2.
Mass Hibsteria Fanzine: £1.

RECORD ATTENDANCE

65,860 v Heart Of Midlothian,1950.

AVERAGE ATTENDANCE

2003-2004: 9,138 (Premier League).

DID YOU KNOW?

That Hibernian was the Roman name for Ireland and maintains a link with the Irish born founders of the Club.

KILMARNOCK

Ground Name: Rugby Park
Capacity: 18,128 (all-seated)
Address: Rugby Park, Kilmarnock KA1 2DP
Telephone No: 01563-545-300
Fax No: 01563-522-181
Pitch Size: 115 x 74 yards
Club Nickname: Killie
Home Kit Colours: Blue, White & Red
Official Website:
www.kilmarnockfc.co.uk
Unofficial Websites:
Killie Fever - www.killiefever.co.uk
Kilmarnock Mad (Footy Mad Network) - www.kilmarnock-mad.co.uk
Killiefc.com - www.killiefc.com

WHAT'S THE GROUND LIKE?

The ground has been transformed with the building of three new stands in the mid 1990s. Both ends of the ground and one side have been redeveloped. The ends are good sized two-tiered stands, which are virtually identical. One of these ends, the Chadwick Stand, is given to away supporters. There are also electric scoreboards placed on the roof of each end. The East Stand on one side of the pitch is also relatively new, and similar in height to the two ends. This stand however, does not run the full length of the pitch. Opposite is the older Main Stand, which dates back to the early 1960s. It is smaller than the other stands and has a fair number of supporting pillars which could obstruct your view. The stadium has unusual looking floodlights protruding from the roofs of the two side stands.

WHAT'S IT LIKE FOR VISITORS?

Away fans are housed in the Chadwick

Stand at one end of the pitch. The facilities and views are generally very good although I have had some fans comment that the legroom is a little tight. David Tennant, a visiting St Mirren supporter, adds: 'A great ground to visit, with friendly supporters, some good pubs and also don't forget to sample their legendary pies'.

WHERE TO DRINK

Gordon Duff recommends the Howard Arms, in Glencairn Square, which is only a few minutes walk away from the ground. Otherwise, the ground is not that far from the town centre where there are plenty of bars to be found.

GETTING THERE & WHERE TO PARK

From the A71, take the A759 towards Kilmarnock. Eventually the ground will appear on your left. Turn left off the A735 into South Hamilton Road and left again into Rugby Road for the ground. The ground is quite well signposted around the town. Street parking.

By Train

Kilmarnock Station is served by trains from Glasgow. The ground is around 15-20 minutes walk from the station. Emerging from the station you will find yourself at the top of John Finnie Street. Walk down this street against the flow of the one-way traffic. At the traffic lights at the bottom of the street (by the Sheriff Court), turn right into Portland Road. Take the second left at the traffic lights into South Hamilton Street and proceed to the first right turn into Rugby Road and the ground.

Thanks to Stephen Millar for providing the directions.

LOCAL RIVALS

Ayr United.

ADMISSION PRICES

Non Old Firm Games:

All areas of the ground:

Adults: £18. Concessions: (OAP'/U16s): £12.

Under 16s can gain admission to the Moffat Stand for £5.

Old Firm Games:

Home Fans: Adults £22. Concessions £12.

Away Fans: Adults £22. No Concessions.

PROGRAMME

Official Programme: £1.50.

RECORD ATTENDANCE

35.995 v Rangers,

Scottish Cup, March 10th, 1962.

AVERAGE ATTENDANCE

2003-2004: 6,966 (Premier League).

DID YOU KNOW?

The Club were founded by a group of cricketers who wanted to pursue another sport in the winter to keep fit. They first played rugby for three years before changing to football. Hence the naming of the ground: Rugby Park.

LIVINGSTON

Ground Name: City Stadium
(still known to many fans as Almondvale)
Capacity: 10,000 (all-seated)
Address: Livingston,
West Lothian
EH54 7DN
Telephone No: 01506-417-000
Fax No: 01506-418-888
Pitch Size: 110 x 76 yards
Club Nickname: Livi Lions
Home Kit Colours: Amber & Black
Official Website:
www.livingstonfc.co.uk
Unofficial Websites:
Livi Fanzine - www.livifanzine.co.uk
Livilions (Rivals Network) - www.livilions.co.uk
Livi Ultras (Footy Mad Network) - www.liviultras.com

WHAT'S THE GROUND LIKE?

This purpose built stadium opened in 1995. It is a small, compact but smart looking ground. All four stands are of roughly the same height and two corners of the ground are filled with covered seating. There are open corners on either side of the West Stand, at one side of the pitch, which also has a few supporting pillars.

George Hobb, a visiting Hearts supporter, adds: 'The Club grew from the ashes of the former Meadowbank Thistle who played in Edinburgh, until in a move similar to NFL franchises, it was moved lock stock and barrel to Livingston. Efforts to retain the name were in vain as the major players saw this as an opportunity to get the town on Scotland's soccer map. What has been achieved in a short time is a minor miracle. Third division to Premier League, crowds quadrupled and most importantly a sound foundation has been put in place. Plus the ground is so neat, that you half expect the players to be on plastic bases and flicked around on the pitch!'

WHAT'S IT LIKE FOR VISITORS?

Away fans are located in the North Stand and the North-East corner of the ground. Up to 4,000 fans can be accommodated in this area. Livingston are a family orientated club and hence you are likely to have an enjoyable and relaxing day out. There is also a small band of drummers and trumpeters in the Livingston crowd who try to raise the atmosphere throughout the game, with a number of well known tunes. Aidan Hegarty, a visiting Dundee United supporter, adds: 'Visitors should be aware that the Club operates a zero tolerance policy towards foul or abusive language, so try to be on your best behaviour'.

WHERE TO DRINK

George Hobbs informs me to try The Granary up from the Main Stand, which was quite popular on his visit. Whilst up at the McArthur Glen Shopping Centre, there is a Wetherspoons pub, although no football colours are allowed.

GETTING THERE & WHERE TO PARK

Livingston is situated approximately 18 miles west of Edinburgh and easily accessible from the M8 motorway. The stadium is fairly well signposted around the town. The following directions from the M8 are not necessarily the quickest, but they are fairly straightforward to follow.

Leave the M8 at Junction 3 and take the A899 towards Livingston. Leave this road when you reach the large roundabout that is the junction with the A71 (Bankton Road). Turn right onto the A71 and at the next island turn right into Alderstone Road (signposted town centre). Go straight across three roundabouts and then turn right at the second set of traffic lights and into the stadium approach road. There is a fair sized car park at the stadium, although it does cost a whopping £5 to park there!

By Train

There are two stations that are in reach of the ground. Livingston North and Livingston South. The North station is served by trains from Edinburgh and is about a 15 minute walk from the ground, whilst the South station has trains from both Edinburgh and Glasgow and is about a 25 minute walk away from the ground.

LOCAL RIVALS

Being a relatively new club, local rivalries have yet to be firmly established. However, if the Club maintains its current growth, then the Edinburgh clubs may be the focus of rivalry.

ADMISSION PRICES

Adults: £17. Concessions: £10.

PROGRAMME

Official Programme: £2.

RECORD ATTENDANCE

10,112 v Rangers, Premier League, October 27th 2001.

AVERAGE ATTENDANCE

2003-2004: 5,117 (Premier League).

DID YOU KNOW?

The smallest attendance recorded for a Livingston league match was just 223, when they attended the game against Queens Park at Meadowbank Stadium in 1995. How times have now changed ...

MOTHERWELL

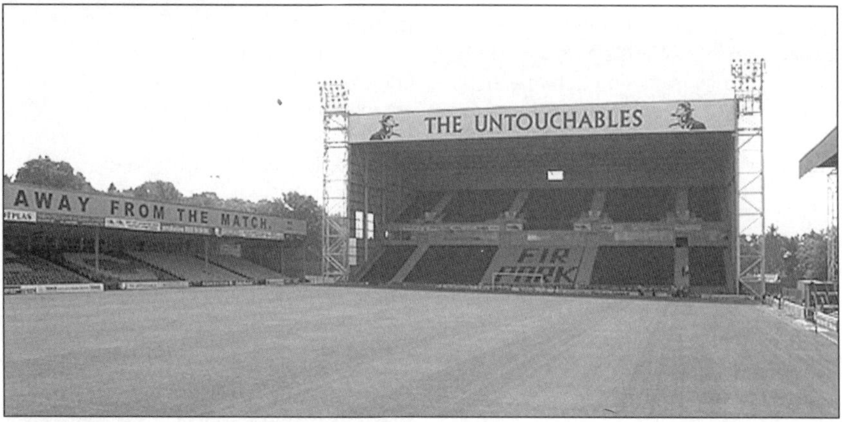

Ground Name: Fir Park
Capacity: 13,742 (all-seated)
Address: Fir Park, Motherwell ML1 2QN
Telephone No: 01698-333-333
Fax No: 01698-276-333
Pitch Size: 110 x 75 yards
Club Nickname: The Well or The Steelmen
Home Kit Colours: Amber & Claret
Official Website:
www.motherwellfc.co.uk
Unofficial Websites:
Well Fever - www.wellfever.co.uk
Motherwellfc.org - www.motherwellfc.org
Well Talk (Sport Network) - www.ebranch.cjb.net

WHAT'S THE GROUND LIKE?

The stadium is dominated by the large South Stand at one end. Almost twice the height of the other stands, it is two-tiered with a row of executive boxes running across the middle. Opposite, the Davie Cooper Stand is a small covered seated stand. The single-tiered Main Stand on one side of the ground is both raised above pitch level and set back from it. This older stand has windshields to either side as well as a few supporting pillars. It is unusual in that the stand itself doesn't run the full length of the pitch, but the supporting steelwork does, making for an odd looking sight. According to Simon Inglis in his book 'The Football Grounds Of Great Britain', this was because it was originally intended in 1962 to build a full length stand but due to a dispute with a house owner beyond the corner of that ground (a dispute which the club lost), it was never completed as intended. This stand was funded chiefly from the sale at that time of no less than Ian St John and Pat Quinn to Liverpool. This did not go down well with the fans as many subsequently boycotted the stand and to this day it is the most sparsely populated section of the ground. Opposite is the smaller East Stand, which also has a number of supporting pillars, running across it.

WHAT'S IT LIKE FOR VISITORS?

Away fans are housed in the South Stand at one end of the pitch. Normally only the lower tier is opened for away fans, but if demand requires it, then the upper tier can be opened also. Up to 5,000 fans can be accommodated in the two tiers. The view of the playing action from this stand is pretty good, as well as the facilities. David Tennant, a visiting St Mirren supporter, adds: 'Overall Fir Park is a good day out. The huge away stand was very nice to be in and the atmosphere was alright. No hassle around the ground, but some good banter was had with the home support.'

WHERE TO DRINK

Craig Barry recommends the 'Jack Daniels Bar', which is the closest to the ground. It is popular with both home and away fans, each having their own bar. Craig Irving adds: 'The Fir Park Social Club is on the same road as the ground and is an extremely friendly boozer. Away fans are normally admitted, although restrictions may be put in place for Old Firm games'.

GETTING THERE & WHERE TO PARK

Leave the M74 at Junction 6 and head towards Motherwell. At the first set of lights, turn right onto the B754 (Airbles Road) towards Wishaw. The ground is at the end of this road on the right. Street parking.

By Train

Airbles station is the closest to the ground, but is only served by a local service. You are more likely to end up instead at Motherwell Central station, which is around a 15 minute walk from the ground. Alan McAulay adds: 'You exit the train station facing the main shopping street in the direction of the ground. Go straight along it through the shopping precinct/centre, past the shopping centre car park, which leads to an underpass. Go through this, up the stairs and turn right. Then go straight on and the large stand gradually comes into view from behind Wilsons Furniture Store. The road forks at this point with away fans, and those going into the old seated terrace, going to the left, and all other fans to the right. Away fans walking from Motherwell should note that the road to the away end is a long and winding one (you think you're there when you see the stand, but it takes about another 5 minutes to reach it), so should allow plenty of time. There is also a pretty good pub right next to Motherwell Central, but fans should remember to leave on time, the last time I was in Motherwell I missed the first 10 minutes!'

LOCAL RIVALS

Airdrie United and Hamilton.

ADMISSION PRICES

Admission prices for home supporters vary depending on the category of match. The Club operate a standard and premium category. Premium prices are shown in brackets:

Main Stand: Adults: £17 (£19). Concessions: £10 (£12). Children: £7 (£8).
East Stand: Adults: £12 (£15). Concessions: £7 (£9). Children: £3 (£6).

Davie Cooper Stand: Adults: £15 (£17). Concessions: £9 (£11). Children: £6 (£7). Adult + 1 child: £20 (£22).
Away Fans: Motorola Stand: Adults: £18 (£19). Concessions: £9 (£11). Children: £6 (£8).

PROGRAMME

Official Programme: £2.

RECORD ATTENDANCE

35,632 v Glasgow Rangers, 1952.

AVERAGE ATTENDANCE

2003-2004: 6,225 (Premier League).

DID YOU KNOW?

The Club are unofficially nicknamed 'The Dossers', which was given by a local paper to the League Championship winning side of 1932, who labelled the laidback passing style of the team as 'those Dossers fae the Shire' (Lanarkshire).

PARTICK THISTLE

Ground Name: Firhill Stadium
Capacity: 13,079 (10,887 seated)
Address: 80 Firhill Road, Glasgow G20 7AL
Telephone No: 0141-579-1971
Fax No: 0141-945-1525
Pitch Size: 111 x 76 yards
Club Nickname: The Jags
Home Kit Colours: Red, Yellow & Black
Official Website: www.ptfc.co.uk
Unofficial Websites:
Over Land & Sea - http://www.chem.gla.ac.uk/~johnm/thistle/partick.html
The Harry Rags - www.theharrywraggs.co.uk
PTFC.net - www.ptfc.net

WHAT'S THE GROUND LIKE?

On one side of the ground is the impressive looking Jackie Husband Stand. This is a large, covered single-tiered stand. Opposite is the older Main Stand, which has raised seating above pitch level. This stand is covered and has a fair few supporting pillars which may obstruct your view. It was originally built in 1927. The stand looks a little odd as the lower end has been given over to what looks like administrative offices. As it is timber framed, smoking is not permitted in the seated area. At the North End of the ground is the new North Stand, which replaced a former open terrace. This all-seated covered stand originally only ran for around two-thirds of the width of the pitch, but has been extended during the summer of 2003, so that it now completely fills that end of the ground. Opposite the South End is a classic looking open terrace, which is semi-circular in shape. Under SPL rules, this terrace cannot be used for League fixtures and therefore will only be used if required for Cup games. The Club do intend to redevelop this end at some point in the future.

WHAT'S IT LIKE FOR VISITORS?

Away fans are primarily housed in the new North Stand at one side of the pitch, where around 2,000 can be accommodated. The view of the playing action and the facilities on offer are pretty good. The best thing about this stand is that a relatively few away supporters can make some noise from it, contributing to a normally good atmosphere within the ground. If demand requires it, then the North part of the older Main Stand can also be allocated to away fans.

Firhill holds a somewhat illustrious personal record for me. Having had a few beers before the game, I unfortunately needed to find the gents halfway through the first half. Just as I went in, up went a roar from inside the ground, Partick had scored. Then on returning, just as I reached the bottom of the stairs, going back up into the stand, Partick scored again! So to this day, this is my personal record for missing two goals with one pee! Of course, I took a fair bit of ribbing from the surrounding supporters as I returned to my seat. In a dull second half, there were plenty of suggestions from the fans around me that perhaps I should work my goal magic by going to the gents again!

Firhill is the only ground that I have visited on my extensive travels that sells Pot Noodles from its refreshment areas (apart from pies etc..).

WHERE TO DRINK

Jim McFarlane recommends the Munn's Vaults on Maryhill Road. This pub is only around a five minute walk from the entrance to the away end and has a good mix of home and away support. Further down Maryhill Road towards the city centre, the Woodside Inn, on the right side of the road, which also welcomes away fans.

GETTING THERE & WHERE TO PARK

From The West:
Leave the M8 at Junction 17 and follow the A81, Maryhill Road towards Maryhill. Turn right into Firhill Road for the ground.
From The East:
Leave the M8 at Junction 16 and follow the A81, Maryhill Road towards Maryhill. Turn right into Firhill Road for the ground.

Street Parking (although don't be surprised if you are approached by a number of kids wanting to 'mind your car, mister?').

By Train/Underground
Maryhill station is the closest train station to the ground, but it is still a fair walk away (20-25 minutes). It is served by trains from Glasgow Queens Street but it may be best instead to use the underground.

By Underground:
Richard Jones informs me: 'You can alight at two or three underground stations. Probably the easiest is to get off at St. Georges Cross and just head North up Maryhill Road until you see the stadium (in Firhill road just off Maryhill road). It should take around 10-15 minutes to walk. Another option is to get off at Kelvinbridge (this is slightly closer to Firhill than St. Georges Cross). Go up the stairs/escalators to Great Western Road, cross Great Western Road and turn to your right. Walk only a few metres until you come to North Woodside Road on your left. Walk down that road until you come to Maryhill Road. Turn left along Maryhill Road to get to the ground.

Alan McAulay adds: 'If you are looking to have a pre-match drink in Byres Road, then get off at Hillhead Underground Station. Most of the pubs are on the left-hand side when you exit the station, although the very student-ish Curlers Bar is right next to it. A better bet may be Tennents Bar, which is further down as it has more of a footy-friendly atmosphere. To then get to the ground from Byres Road turn right out of Hillhead Station and go straight along past the library and Fopp records, then turn right again. Kelvinbridge station is on your right-hand side, but below street level, so keep an eye out for it'. From there, follow the directions as above.

LOCAL RIVALS

Clyde, Airdrie, St Mirren.

ADMISSION PRICES

Seating: Adults: £16*. Concessions: £8
Terrace (only open for big cup games): Adults: £13. Concessions £6.

*For all ticket games this rises to £19.

PROGRAMME

Official Programme: £2.

RECORD ATTENDANCE

49,838 v Rangers (1922).

AVERAGE ATTENDANCE

2003-2004: 4,710 (Premier League).

DID YOU KNOW?

That Firhill is the closest League Football Ground to Glasgow City Centre.

Please note that at the time of going to print it was still unclear as to which division Partick will be playing in for the 2004/05 season. At the time of writing First Division Champions Inverness are currently appealing against a decision not to admit them to the SPL (their ground currently does not meet SPL criteria). If the outcome of the appeal results in Inverness being promoted then Partick who finished bottom of the SPL last season will play in Division One for the 2004/05 season. If the appeal is overturned then Partick will remain in the Premier League.

RANGERS

Ground Name: Ibrox Stadium
Capacity: 50,411 (all-seated)
Address: 150 Edmiston Drive, Glasgow, G51 2XD
Telephone No: 0870-600-1972
Fax No: 0870-600-1978
Ticket Office: 0870-600-1993
Pitch Size: 115 x 78 yards
Club Nickname: The Gers or Teddy Bears
Home Kit Colours: Blue, Red & White
Official Website: www.rangers.co.uk
Unofficial Websites:
GersNet - www.gersnet.com
Follow, Follow (Footy Mad Network) - www.followfollow.com

WHAT'S THE GROUND LIKE?

The ground was mostly redeveloped in the late 1970s and early 1980s with three new stands being constructed. Only the Main Stand (which was originally built in 1929) at one side of the pitch remains of the old Ibrox. This stand has also been refurbished and in 1994 a third tier was added to it. The impressive red brick facade of this stand was left intact (it is a listed building), which means that the ground has a great blend of modern facilities, whilst still retaining its historic character. The three relatively new stands are all good sized and two-tiered. On either side of the Govan Stand, the corners have been filled, with seating in the lower tier and large video screens in the upper tier. Even though the Main Stand is larger than the other stands, the ground looks well balanced as the roof comes down to the same height as the others. The corners to either side of this stand are partly open, being filled with stairwells. There are also a couple of small electric scoreboards at either end of the ground. Overall, a superb ground that is arguably one of the best in Britain.

FUTURE GROUND DEVELOPMENTS

The Club have proposed plans to add a third tier to the Govan Stand. This would boost the capacity to around 58,000.

However, as of yet, no firm timescales have been announced for this development to take place.

WHAT'S IT LIKE FOR VISITORS?

Away fans are located in the lower tier of the Broomloan Stand, towards the Govan Stand and the bulk are located in this corner of the ground, below one of the large video screens. Its facilities are fairly good, as well as enjoying a decent view of the playing action. For big games such as the Old Firm derby, the whole of the Broomloan Stand can be allocated to the away support. Although the ground itself is great, I found Ibrox to be quite intimidating. I would advise that you exercise caution around the ground and to keep club colours covered.

Although most games sell out at Ibrox, tickets can be bought for most games, as long as you call the ticket office at least a couple of weeks prior to the fixture.

WHERE TO DRINK

Most bars around the vicinity of the ground are normally very crowded and not particularly away fan friendly, so it may be an idea to drink in the city centre before moving onto the ground. However, The Albion on Broomloan Road by the ground has been recommended by some away fans.

James Prentice adds: 'Away supporters tend to head for bars towards the Centre of Glasgow, as there is less chance of any hassle then when around the ground. For Rangers fans, there are several good bars to be found around Ibrox. There is the District Bar on Paisley Road West, which is an excellent, typical Glaswegian pub, and the Louden Bar, which is just around the corner - a Rangers fan's heaven and a real Rangers pub. The Stadium Bar on Copland Road is OK. There are also chip shops and a plethora of chips and burger vans around the ground on matchdays, as would be expected. Also, there is a relatively new café in a car park opposite Ladbrokes' Bookmakers on Copland Road which serves good meals at cheap prices'.

GETTING THERE & WHERE TO PARK

Leave the M8 at Junction 23 and head towards Govan/Clyde Tunnel on the A8 Paisley Road West. You will come to the stadium on your right after about a mile and a half. The roads around Ibrox become pretty congested, so allow some

extra time for your journey. Street parking.

By Train/Underground

The ground is at least a couple of miles away from Glasgow Central and Queens Street railway stations. Either take a taxi or proceed down Argyll Street to the St. Enoch Underground Station and take the Inner Circle underground train to the ground. Ibrox has its own underground station, only a few minutes walk away. The station though gets exceptionally busy after the games. Alternatively, there always seems to be a number of buses running by the ground which are heading back into the city centre.

James Prentice adds: 'Ibrox underground has huge queues after games and some supporters may prefer to use Cessnock underground station on Paisley Road West, as fewer people seem to use it on a match day. Turn out of the stadium and go left on to Edminston Drive, and the station is about five minutes walk away after the road joins up with Paisley Road West (adult single tickets are about 80p). While it is a tiny bit longer to walk to Cessnock, you may well stand a better chance of getting on the underground quicker than at Ibrox. Buses also run along Paisley Road West and can take you right into the city centre every few minutes. Getting off at Bridge Street is about 90p single and is a two minute walk over the River Clyde for the centre of Glasgow'. Otherwise if you are feeling particularly brave you can embark on the 40 minute walk back to the city centre.

LOCAL RIVALS

Celtic.

ADMISSION PRICES

Home Fans:

Main Stand Club Deck: Adults £22.
Main Stand Front: Adults £22.
Main Stand Rear: Adults £17.
Govan Stand (Upper Tier): Adults: £22.
Govan Stand (Lower Tier): Adults £18.
Broomloan Stand (Upper Tier): Adults £18.
Broomloan Stand (Lower Tier): Adults £17.
Copland Stand (Upper Tier): Adults £18.
Copland Stand (Lower Tier): Adults £17.
Under 16s (all areas): £11.
Over 65s (all areas) £13.

Away Fans:

Broomloan Stand (Lower Tier): Adults: £17. Over 65s: £13. Under 16s £11.

PROGRAMME & FANZINE

Official Programme: £2 - Contains quite a few pages of adverts.
Fanzine: Follow, Follow £1.50.

RECORD ATTENDANCE

118,567 v Celtic, 1939.

AVERAGE ATTENDANCE

2003-2004: 48,992 (Premier League).

STADIUM TOURS

The Club offer tours on Mondays, Fridays and Sundays. The tour lasts around 90 minutes and costs £7 for adults and £5 concessions. Tours can be booked by calling 0870 600 1972.

DID YOU KNOW?

That ground name of Ibrox was taken from the name of a district in Glasgow.

SCOTTISH FIRST, SECOND AND THIRD DIVISIONS

are arranged in **alphabetical order** on pages 36 - 95

AIRDRIE UNITED

Ground Name: Excelsior Stadium (although most Airdrie fans call it New Broomfield)
Capacity: 10,171 (all-seated)
Address: 60 St Enoch Square, Glasgow G1 4AG
Telephone No: 07710-230775
Fax No: 0141-221-1497
Pitch Size: 115 x 75 yards
Club Nickname: Diamonds
Home Kit Colours: White, Red & Black
Official Website: www.airdrieunitedfc.com
Unofficial Website: Broomfield Stomp (Sport Network) - www.sportnetwork.net/main/s2.htm

WHAT'S THE GROUND LIKE?

The Club are the League's 'newcomers' having been formed in June 2002, after Airdrieonians went out of business. Following a successful takeover of Clydebank, the new Airdrie United have taken their place in the league. Unsurprisingly Airdrie are housed at the same ground where Aidrieonians played. It opened in August 1998.

It is a smart looking all-seated stadium comprising four separate, single-tiered, covered stands. The Jack Dalziel Stand, (named after a former Airdrieonians Chairman) at one side of the pitch, is the largest of the four stands. Impressive looking, it has a row of executive boxes running across the back. The other three stands are of an equal height which gives the ground a balanced look. The corners of the ground are open, apart from the tall floodlights.

WHAT'S IT LIKE FOR VISITORS?

The modern ground is certainly an excellent one and the facilities available are not bad. However, the atmosphere generated within the ground can be quite lacking at times. For most games the ground is only a quarter full and just a couple of stands (and for some games only one stand) are open. It would be great to return to this ground to see a game in front of a full house, as that would do it justice.

Away fans are normally located in the East Stand at one side of the pitch. Dependant on away numbers, you may find only the portion of the West Stand allocated (this stand is shared with home supporters) or just the East Stand, or both. In the event that the Club were to draw one of the Old Firm sides, then the Club would give their maximum allocation of away seats (6,500), comprising all of the stadium, apart from the West Stand.

WHERE TO DRINK

There is a supporters' bar at the ground, within the Jack Dalziel Stand. Otherwise, as John McCleod informs me: 'The nearest pub is the Albert which is a good 10 minutes walk away from the ground'.

GETTING THERE & WHERE TO PARK

Leave the M8 at Junction 6, the Newhouse Junction, and take the A73 towards Cumbernauld. After two miles turn right into Petersburn Road (B8058) and you will see the ground over on the left. There is a fair sized car park at the ground, which costs £2. Away fans have their own entrance to the car park, which is signposted on approaching the ground. Chris Cobb adds: 'Allow extra time for your journey as the access roads around Airdrie do tend to get quite clogged up'.

By Train

The closest station to the ground is Drumgeloch, which is around a 5-10 minute walk away. Gary Sneddon provides these directions: 'Come out of the station and turn right and then right again, which takes you over the bridge across the railway. Follow Crowood Drive down the hill and then right into Bankhead Avenue. Follow this road around to the left and then take a right at the first crossroads into Willow Drive. Follow this road around to the right until you reach the shops then take first left into Craigneuk Avenue. The ground is at the bottom of this road on the left hand side. Please note that Airdrie station is a good 20-minute walk away from the ground'.

LOCAL RIVALS

Albion Rovers, Hamilton and Motherwell.

ADMISSION PRICES

Adults: £12.
Children/Senior Citizens: £5.

PROGRAMME

Official Programme: £1.50.

RECORD ATTENDANCE

5,709 v Morton,
Division Two, May 15th 2004.

AVERAGE ATTENDANCE

2003-2004: 1,861 (Division Two)

DID YOU KNOW?

The stadium gets its name from Excelsior FC, who were formed in 1878 and later became known as Airdrieonians.

ALBION ROVERS

Ground Name: Cliftonhill Stadium
Capacity: 2,496 (Seated 489)
Address: Main St, Coatbridge, Lanarkshire ML5 3RB
Telephone No: 01236-606-334
Fax No: 01236-606-334
Pitch Size: 110 x 72 yards
Club Nickname: Wee Rovers
Home Kit Colours: Yellow & Red
Official Website: None at present
Unofficial Websites:
Albionrovers.com - www.albionrovers.com
Unofficial Albion Rovers - www.albionroversfc.tk

WHAT'S THE GROUND LIKE?

The ground is not one of the better in the League, having only a small Main Stand and covered terrace at either side, with both ends being totally open and not used for spectators. The Main Stand is a strange looking affair, as at some point it has had an extension placed on the front of its roof. It has wooden seating to the rear and terracing to the front, with several supporting pillars which may impede your view. Opposite is the small, covered Albion Street Terrace, running about half the length of the pitch. Again, this simple stand has several supporting pillars. There is a cinder track that runs around the playing surface and at one time the ground was also used for speedway meetings.

FUTURE DEVELOPMENTS

Albion have announced their intentions to leave Cliftonville and move to a new 3,000 capacity ground. The Club are currently investigating possible locations for the new stadium, including one at Whifflet. It is close to the site of the old Rovers ground which they played at between 1884 and 1919 before they moved to Cliftonville. The proceeds of the sale of Cliftonville would be used to finance the new ground.

WHAT'S IT LIKE FOR VISITORS

Crowd segregation is not in force for most games. If it is imposed, then part of the Main Stand and Albion Street Terrace are given to away supporters. Stefan, a visiting fan from Germany, provides the following: 'When I was there, they played East Stirlingshire. There was no trouble at all with visiting fans and the fans of both clubs were mixed in together in the Main Stand. The stand itself had a nice small bar at the back, which I enjoyed before the game. On the whole there was a very welcoming atmosphere at Cliftonhill'.

WHERE TO DRINK

Michael Cooper informs me: "There is a bar at the stadium itself which is aptly named 'The Rovers Return'. Otherwise the nearest pub to the stadium is called 'Big Owens Bar'. Away fans are welcome in both of these'. Big Owens Bar can be found further down the A89 towards Airdrie, by the fire station.

GETTING THERE & WHERE TO PARK

Leave the M74 at Junction 5 at take the A725 towards Coatbridge. Continue on the A725 into the centre of Coatbridge and on reaching a large traffic island (where you can see the floodlights of the ground on the right), turn right onto the A89 towards Airdrie. The ground is a short distance down this road on the left. Street Parking.

By Train

The nearest railway stations are Coatdyke and Whifflet, which are both about a ten-minute walk away from the ground.

LOCAL RIVALS

Airdrie United.

ADMISSION PRICES

Seating:

Adults: £8. Concessions: £4. Children Free (when accompanied by an adult).

Terrace:

Adults: £7. Concessions: £3. Children Free (when accompanied by an adult).

PROGRAMME

Official Programme: £1.

RECORD ATTENDANCE

27,381 v Glasgow Rangers, Scottish Cup 2nd Round, February 8th, 1936.

AVERAGE ATTENDANCE

2003-2004: 348 (Division Three).

DID YOU KNOW?

The current Main Stand was originally built in 1920.

ALLOA ATHLETIC

Ground Name: Recreation Park
Capacity: 3,100 (400 seated)
Address: Clackmannan Rd, Alloa, FK10 1RY
Telephone No: 01259-722-695
Fax No: 01259-210-886
Pitch Size: 110 x 75 yards
Club Nickname: Wasps
Home Kit Colours: Gold & Black
Official Website:
www.alloaathletic.co.uk
Unofficial Website:
The Duffle -
www.geocities.com/alloa_athletic/

WHAT'S THE GROUND LIKE?

The ground is predominantly open terracing, with terraces behind each goal and along one side of the pitch. There is an unusual looking Main Stand on the other side of the ground. This covered all-seated stand runs for around half the length of the pitch. The seating is raised above pitch level and there are a number of supporting pillars, plus a couple of floodlight pylons which could impede your view. Opposite there is a small covered area in the middle of the terrace towards the rear. Again it has a number of supporting pillars running across the front of it, with a row of four floodlight pylons in front, running along the perimeter of the pitch.

WHAT'S IT LIKE FOR VISITORS?

Segregation of supporters is not normally in force for most league games. When segregation has been imposed before, away fans have been placed in the Clackmannan Road Terrace at one end of the ground and/or the Hilton Road Terrace running down one side of the pitch. Both these terraces are uncovered, so be prepared to get wet. Normally a relaxing and enjoyable visit.

WHERE TO DRINK

There are no bars in the immediate vicinity of the ground. Duncan Condie tells me: 'I believe that The Bank and The Thistle are good pubs for a pre-match drink. Both are in the town centre about 5-10 minutes walk along Clackmannan Road'.

GETTING THERE & WHERE TO PARK

The ground is easy to find and it is located on the A907, on the West side of town. If approaching from Stirling, continue on the A907 through the centre of Alloa and you will eventually reach the ground on your left. Street parking.

By Train

The nearest station is in Stirling which is around seven miles away.

LOCAL RIVALS

Stirling Albion.

ADMISSION PRICES

Seating:

Adults: £10. Concessions: £6.

Terrace:

Adults: £9. Concessions: £5.

PROGRAMME

Official Programme: £1.50.

RECORD ATTENDANCE

13,000 v Dunfermline Athletic
Scottish Cup, 3rd Round replay, February 26th, 1939.

AVERAGE ATTENDANCE

2003-2004: 589 (Division Two).

DID YOU KNOW?

Floodlights were first used at the ground in the 1979-80 season.

ARBROATH

Ground Name: Gayfield Park
Capacity: 6,488 (seated 714)
Address: Arbroath,
Angus, DD11 1QB
Telephone No: 01241-872-157
Fax No: 01241-431-125
Pitch Size: 115 x 71 yards
Club Nickname: Red Lichties
Home Kit Colours: Maroon & White
Official Website:
www.arbroathfc.co.uk
Unofficial Websites:
Lichties News - www.arbroathfc.org.uk
Arbroath Mad (Footy Mad Network) - www.arbroath-mad.co.uk

WHAT'S THE GROUND LIKE?

Gayfield is predominantly made up of terracing which extends around three corners of the ground. However, this gives the stadium a lot of character, especially as terracing is slowly but surely disappearing generally from football stadia. On one side is the new Gayfield Main Stand, opened in 2002. This is a covered single-tiered, all-seated stand. The other sides of the ground are all terraces that are of a similar size. Each side has a small covered area which is over the centre part of the terraces to the rear. There are also a number of small floodlight pylons that run down the East side of the pitch, the bases of which are situated within the East Terrace.

WHAT'S IT LIKE FOR VISITORS?

Supporters are normally housed in the Seaforth Terrace at one end of the ground. This end is also affectionately known as the 'Pleash End' as it has the Pleasureland indoor amusement arcade at the back of it. If demand requires, then the East Terrace at one side of the pitch can also be allocated. Normally a relaxed and hassle free day out. John Stenhouse adds: 'Make sure you have a pie, they are amongst the best you'll find'.

Jamie Malley informs me: "No matter how good the weather forecast is take a coat! And if it's anytime between October and March also take a set of thermals. Gayfield is the closest ground to the sea in Britain (and in fact in Europe) and when the wind comes in off the North Sea it gets a wee bit chilly. Also if it's really windy don't stand in the East terrace unless you've got an umbrella - the sea may come over the wall and you'll end up very wet!'

WHERE TO DRINK

The nearest bar to the ground is the Tutties Neuk, on Queens Drive, which is just across the road from the ground. The bar is popular with both home and away fans, although it is a little on the small side.

Jamie Malley adds: 'Tutties is the place to go pre-match. Home and away supporters will freely mingle before the game and the banter is pretty good - I've even heard some away fans describe this as the best pre-match boozer in Scotland. Otherwise, within the town itself, there are a number of pubs, the best of which is probably the Corn Exchange for cheap beer 'n' food. If you are after a quieter pub, the harbour area has a load. For food the pies at Gayfield are so-so and if you want one, best go before half-time as they usually run out. Remember Arbroath is famous for its fish, so make sure you have some fish and chips before you leave. If there's a chippie that serves better and fresher fish than Peppos on the harbour, then I've yet to find it and I've eaten fish & chips all over the country! Also if you are down at the harbour there's no end of shops selling Smokies'.

GETTING THERE & WHERE TO PARK

The ground is easy to find as it is located on the main A92. If approaching Arbroath on the A92 from the South, you will come to the ground on your right. There is plenty of street parking to be found along the sea front.

By Train

Arbroath train station is around a 15 minute walk away from the ground. From the railway station come out of the main entrance and turn left. Walk down to the bottom of this road and turn right into Milgate Loan. The ground is approximately half a mile along this road - you can't miss it.

From the Bus Station

Come out of the bus station onto the dual carriageway - turn right and walk away from the town towards the Signal Tower museum. You'll see the ground ahead of you – it's a 10-15 minute walk.

Thanks to Jamie Malley for providing the directions.

LOCAL RIVALS

Montrose, Forfar and Brechin.

ADMISSION PRICES

Seating:
Adults: £10. Juvenile/OAP: £5.
Terracing:
Adult: £9. Juvenile/OAP: £5.
Parent + Child: £11.

PROGRAMME

Official Programme: £1.50.

RECORD ATTENDANCE

13,510 v Rangers, February 22nd, 1952.

AVERAGE ATTENDANCE

2003-2004: 625 (Division Two).

DID YOU KNOW?

That Arbroath hold the world record for the biggest victory in a competitive game. 36-0, against Aberdeen Bon Accord in 1885.

AYR UNITED

Ground Name: Somerset Park
Capacity: 10,243 (seated 1,549)
Address: Tryfield Place, Ayr KA8 9NB
Telephone No: 01292-263-435
Fax No: 01292-281-314
Pitch Size: 110 x 72 yards
Club Nickname: The Honest Men
Home Kit Colours: White & Black
Official Website: None at present
Unofficial Website:
The Honest Page - www.honestpage.co.uk

WHAT'S THE GROUND LIKE?

A classic traditional looking ground that is predominantly terracing. Only one side has a seating area, in the old Main Stand, part of which dates back to 1924. This stand is covered and the seated area is raised above pitch level. There are also a few supporting pillars which can spoil the view. This stand was extended sideways in 1989. In front of the stand are some small sections of terracing, the team dugouts and a small conservatory type structure, which looked to be used by the police. On the other side is a large open terrace which extends around the corners of the ground. This area is split between home and away fans who are segregated by a large fence running down the middle of it. At the back of the home fans section is a strange concrete box like structure that looks to have been built behind the existing terrace. This appears to house a number of hospitality boxes that overlook the ground. Both ends are quite similar looking, as they are of roughly the same size and both are covered terracing. The home end, the Somerset Road end, is a partly covered (to the rear) medium sized terrace, that has a row of supporting pillars running across the front of it. Away fans are located in the opposite end in the Railway Terrace. The ground is completed with a striking set of four floodlight pylons, one located at each corner of the ground.

WHAT'S IT LIKE FOR VISITORS?

Away fans are primarily located in the covered Railway End Terrace at one end of the ground, as well as some open terrace to either side of it. So visiting fans have a choice as to whether to view the action from either an end or side of the pitch and, unless there is a huge travelling support, you will normally get a good view of the playing action. With the away end being covered, a relatively small number of away fans can really create some noise, adding to the atmosphere. There are two refreshment kiosks in the away section serving the usual array of pies, hot dogs and burgers. Unfortunately, though, there is only one set of toilets that are right by the entrance turnstiles to the away end. I would have to say that the men's urinals looked as if they dated back to when the ground opened. I did notice on my visit that parts of the open terrace had a fair few white blobs all over them, thanks to the large local population of seagulls. It may be an idea to make sure you wear a hat if you use the open terrace!

Simon Lyndsay, a visiting Falkirk supporter, adds: 'This is my favourite away game. It is a great old fashioned ground with good pubs, pies, great fish and chips and I have never had a bit of bother there. The fans can have a go at one another during the game (loads of verbals), but walking away at the end, there never seems to be any hassle. An enthusiastic two thumbs up from me for Somerset Park'.

WHERE TO DRINK

There are no bars in the immediate vicinity of the ground. The nearest I could find was the 'The Prince Of Wales' which is about a five minute walk away. It is a fair sized comfortable bar with a large screen television showing SKY Sports. This bar is situated on the A719 (Whitletts Road) going towards Ayr town centre. Otherwise, the town centre is about ten minutes walk away from the ground, where there are plenty of good bars to be found.

GETTING THERE & WHERE TO PARK

From the A77, take the A719 (Whitletts Road) into Ayr. After passing the racecourse on your left, turn right at the next set of traffic lights for the ground, or turn left to take you down to an unofficial car park. Turning right will take you into Burnett Terrace, then left into Hawkhill Avenue and then right into Somerset Road. The ground is down on the left. There is plenty of parking to be found around the ground.

By Train

The closest station is Newton-on-Ayr but not many trains stop at this station. You will probably end up at Ayr station which is about ten minutes walk from the ground.

LOCAL RIVALS

Kilmarnock.

ADMISSION PRICES

Seating:

Adults: £13.50 and £15. Concessions: £6.50.

Terrace:

Adults: £10. Concessions: £5.

PROGRAMME

Official Programme: £2.

RECORD ATTENDANCE

25,225 v Rangers, 1969.

AVERAGE ATTENDANCE

2003-2004: 1,706 (Division One).

DID YOU KNOW?

The Club's nickname comes from a line in a famous poem called Tam O'Shanter by Robert Burns: 'Auld Ayr, wham ne'er a town surpasses, for "honest men" and bonny lasses'.

BERWICK RANGERS

Ground Name: Shielfield Park
Capacity: 4,131 (seated 1,366)
Address: Tweedmouth, Berwick-upon-Tweed TD15 2EF
Telephone No: 01289-307-424
Fax No: 01289-307-424
Pitch Size: 110 x 70 yards
Club Nickname: The Borderers
Home Kit Colours: Gold & Black
Official Website: None at present
Unofficial Websites:
The Ducket - www.theducket.com
Berwick Rangers Online (Footy Mad Network) - www.berwickrangers-mad.co.uk/

WHAT'S THE GROUND LIKE?

The ground is a classic oval shape, with a cinder track surrounding the playing area (which is used by the Berwick Bandits Speedway Team during the summer). Both ends are small open terraces, whilst on one side is the Main Stand. This small all-seated stand is covered, but has a row of floodlights running across the front of the stand, the foundations of which could impede your view. Opposite is another mostly open terrace. However there is a small covered area, known as the 'Ducket Enclosure', which straddles the halfway line.

WHAT'S IT LIKE FOR VISITORS?

Supporters are not normally segregated at Shielfield. If segregation needs to be enforced then the Main Stand can be split between home and away supporters. If necessary, such as a visit by one of the old firm sides, then all of the terracing can be allocated. As Bill Purvis says; 'Visiting supporters can enjoy a relaxed atmosphere and friendly banter both in the ground and in some of the local hostelries before the match. We do take exception however to being called "English ********" especially as most of the team and half the support are Scots'!

WHERE TO DRINK

Nick Vagg informs me; 'There is the Black & Gold pub adjacent to the ground which is popular with both home and away fans. It has been recently refurbished and has a big screen to show SKY Sports'. Bill Purvis adds; 'Otherwise, coming into the ground by car on the B6354 (see directions) you will pass the Grove which is always popular with both sets of supporters. If you are walking from the Railway Station you will pass several pubs most of which are not too bad, however, once you cross the River Tweed into Tweedmouth you will come upon the Angel Inn on your left which has plenty of Berwick football memorabilia adorning its walls and is a favourite haunt of the home support. After the Match many go to "Barrels Alehouse" which is a well known pub situated at the Berwick end of the Old Bridge'.

GETTING THERE & WHERE TO PARK

From The North:
From the A1 go around Berwick and continue crossing the River Tweed. Then take the left turn towards Spittal (B6354). After about one mile, you will reach the entrance to the ground on your left.
From The South:
From the A1, take the right turn towards Spittal (B6354). After about one mile, you will reach the entrance to the ground on your left.

There is plenty of free car parking available at the ground.

By Train
Berwick station is around a 20 minute walk away from the ground.

'As you leave the station car park, turn right and follow the road around to the left (the opposite direction to the traffic flow on a one-way street). Turn right into Castlegate (this is the main road in to town). Go under the archway of the old town walls and you will come across a mini-roundabout that is opposite to the bus station. Turn right and cross the Royal Tweed Bridge. You are now in Tweedmouth. At the other end of the bridge just follow the road as it curves around to the left, passing a school and a Co-op Superstore. Just after that you will come across a railway viaduct. Turn right here into Shielfield Terrace and the ground is 150-200 yards down on your right.

Thanks to Colin Wallace for providing the above directions.

LOCAL RIVALS

Bill Purvis informs me: 'Matches against Stranraer are jokingly known as Border derbies although it is probably somewhere around 190 miles between the two towns!'

ADMISSION PRICES

Adults: £10. Children and OAPs: £5.

PROGRAMME

Official Programme: £1.50.

RECORD ATTENDANCE

13,365 v Glasgow Rangers,
Scottish Cup 1st Round, January 28th 1967. (Berwick Won 1-0).

AVERAGE ATTENDANCE

2003-2004: 521 (Division Two).

DID YOU KNOW?

That the Club are the only English based Club to play in the Scottish League.

BRECHIN CITY

Ground Name: Glebe Park
Capacity: 3,960 (seated 1,519)
Address: Trinity Rd, Brechin, Angus DD9 6BJ
Telephone No: 01356-622-856
Fax No: 01356-625524
Pitch Size: 110 x 67 yards
Club Nickname: The City
Home Kit Colours: Red & White
Official Website:
www.brechincity.co.uk
Unofficial Website:
Brechin City Mad (Footy Mad Network) - www.brechincity-mad.co.uk

WHAT'S THE GROUND LIKE?

It is a long time since I have visited a ground with such charm and character as Glebe Park. The Main Stand is overlooked by a church spire, whilst opposite a tall, well tended hedge borders the entire length of the open side. This side has a small open terrace only a couple of steps high and there are a number of floodlight pylons running down the front of it. The Main Stand is a small all-seated and covered stand, which straddles the halfway line. You would think at first glance that this was quite an old stand, especially as it has a floodlight protruding from its roof, but in actual fact it was built in 1981 and replaced a similar looking wooden stand. At one end is the Cemetery End terrace, which is covered and has a number of supporting pillars. Opposite, is the latest addition to the ground, the smart looking Trinity Road Stand. Built in the early 1990s, it is a covered all-seated stand, which seats nearly 1,000 spectators. It is unusual, in that it is setback some distance from the pitch and sits upon a raised bank.

WHAT'S IT LIKE FOR VISITORS?

The ground is a pleasure to visit and a friendly welcome awaits most visitors. It is maintained to a high standard and the staff and fans have real pride in their club. If you get the chance, make your way to the rear of the Cemetery Terrace, where in true

Hollywood style, supporters have been invited to have individual plaques with their names inscribed set in concrete. Plus the supporters have also been allowed to place their hand prints in the concrete, giving it that Hollywood look. Supporters are not normally segregated for games and both sets of fans tend to try ousting one another in the Cemetery End. If fans are to be segregated, say for a big cup game, then away fans will normally find that the Trinity Road Stand has been allocated to them. Neil Stapleton adds: 'If you get a chance, sample the soup on sale inside the ground, it is excellent'.

WHERE TO DRINK

Lennie Johnson informs me: 'Visiting supporters are welcome at the City Club, in Southesk Street, which is only a short walk from Glebe Park. It is a good spot for a pint and their bar lunches are excellent. To find the Club, come out of the main entrance to the ground and turn left down Trinity Road. Turn left at the roundabout by Safeways into Southesk Street. Walk down this street and you will come to the Club on the corner of Commercial Street'. Whilst Calum MacLennan adds: 'There is also the Stables Bar which is good for a pre-match pint. This is only a five minute walk away from the ground. As you come out of the ground entrance, turn left and go down to the roundabout. Go straight across the roundabout and at McConnachys Tyre Centre turn right and the pub is just there'.

GETTING THERE & WHERE TO PARK

From the A90, take the B966 towards Brechin (if coming from the South, ignore the first Brechin turn off on the A90 - the A935, and continue Northwards). Continue along the B966 and you will come to the ground on your left. The entrance is quite small between some houses and is indicated by a small Glebe Park sign. There is a small free car park at the ground which holds around 50 vehicles, otherwise street parking.

By Train

There is no train station in Brechin itself. The nearest station is in Montrose which is eight miles away. You can either then take a taxi to the ground or catch a bus to Brechin.

LOCAL RIVALS

Montrose, Forfar.

ADMISSION PRICES

Seating:

Adults: £12. Parent and Child: £13. Parent and 2 Children: £14. OAPs/Juveniles: £6.

Terrace:

Adults: £11. OAPs/Juveniles: £6.

PROGRAMME

Official Programme: £1.50.

RECORD ATTENDANCE

8,122 v Aberdeen,
Scottish Cup 3rd Round, February 3rd 1973.

AVERAGE ATTENDANCE

2003-2004: 813 (Division One).

DID YOU KNOW?

Glebe Park is the only football ground in Europe which has a hedge surrounding its perimeter.

CLYDE

Ground Name: Broadwood Stadium
Capacity: 8,029 (all-seated)
Address: Ardgoil Drive
Cumbernauld
G68 9NE
Telephone No: 01236-451-511
Fax No: 01236-733-490
Pitch Size: 112 x 76 yards
Club Nickname: Bully Wee
Home Kit Colours: White, Red & Black
Official Website: www.clydefc.co.uk
Unofficial Website:
Clyde Mad (Footy Mad network) - www.clyde-mad.co.uk

WHAT'S THE GROUND LIKE?

The ground was opened in 1995, after a period of ground sharing with Hamilton and Partick Thistle, following their leaving their old Shawfield ground in 1986. The ground has only three sides, the North End being unused. These stands are single-tiered, have windshields to either side and are all-seated and covered. The size of the stands is roughly of the same height, although the Main Stand at one side of the pitch is slightly taller than the other two. This stand has some enclosed corporate seating at the back.

FUTURE GROUND DEVELOPMENTS

Currently the stadium does not comply with Scottish Premier League (SPL) criteria, as it does not have a minimum capacity of 10,000 seats. If Clyde were to gain promotion to the SPL they would have to look at ground sharing with another club, as was recently proposed with Kilmarnock. With the Club coming very close to winning the First Division last season, they have been looking at the feasibility of building a fourth stand at the North End of the stadium. However, there are rumours that the SPL may reduce entry criteria for the 2005-06 season, in which case the scheme to build a fourth stand is likely to be put on hold.

WHAT'S IT LIKE FOR VISITORS?

Away supporters are housed in the West Stand at one side of the pitch. The view of the playing action and the facilities within the stand are both pretty good. The empty North part of the ground provides pleasant views of the Campsie Hills, but can also allow a biting cold wind to enter the ground, so make sure you wrap up well.

In fact some visiting fans have nicknamed the ground 'Ice Station Broadwood'. Still if you need some central heating, then the pies are pretty good. The atmosphere can be a bit flat at times. In an attempt to liven things up, when Clyde score, then 'Song 2' by Blur blasts out around the ground.

WHERE TO DRINK

Ronnie Wallace, a visiting Airdrie supporter, informs me: 'There is a Brewers Fayre pub/restaurant near to the ground off the Craiglinn roundabout. There are other pubs in the neighbouring housing estate of Balloch; however, finding them (or finding your way back!) in the maze of pedestrian walkways can prove quite challenging'. Otherwise in the nearby village of Condorrat there is the Masonic Arms pub. To find this pub, from the front of the stadium go up to the roundabout and turn right, then left at the next roundabout. The pub is just on your left as you enter the village.

GETTING THERE & WHERE TO PARK

The ground is situated on the outskirts of Cumbernauld, just off the A80 Stirling Road. The ground is well signposted from the A80 and there is a good sized car park at the ground, which is free.

By Train

The nearest station is Croy which is about a 20 minute walk away from the ground. This station is served by trains from Glasgow Queens Street.

LOCAL RIVALS

Partick Thistle.

ADMISSION PRICES

Adults: £13. Concessions: £6. Parent + 1 Child: £16.

PROGRAMME

Official Programme: £2.

RECORD ATTENDANCE

At Broadwood:
7,359 v Celtic, August 14th, 1996.
At Shawfield:
52,000 v Rangers Division I, 21 Nov 1908.

AVERAGE ATTENDANCE

2003-2004: 1,672 (Division One).

DID YOU KNOW?

That Broadwood is the highest league ground in Scotland (in terms of being above sea level).

COWDENBEATH

Ground Name: Central Park
Capacity: 5,268 (seated 1,622)
Address: Cowdenbeath, Fife KY4 9QQ
Telephone No: 01383-610-166
Fax No: 01383-512-132
Pitch Size: 107 x 66 yards
Club Nickname: Cowden or Blue Brazil
Home Kit Colours: Royal Blue & White
Official Website:
www.cowdenbeathfc.com
Unofficial Websites:
Supporters Club - www.cowdenbeath.free-online.co.uk/suppclub
Cowdenbeath.net - www.cowdenbeath.net

WHAT'S THE GROUND LIKE?

The ground is also used from time to time for motor sport events. This means that around the oval grass football playing area, at the front of the spectator areas, there is a fair sized tarmac track, plus a meshed safety fence. It is largely an open stadium with three sides having small open terraces. Only on the North Side of the stadium is there a covered Main Stand. Or really I should say Main Stands as there are two, as an older and newer structure, sit side by side. This is because the original old Main Stand was partly destroyed by fire in 1992 and a new structure was constructed beside the remnants of the old stand. Both are covered and all-seated and have a row of floodlight pylons at the front of them, which could affect your view.

WHAT'S IT LIKE FOR VISITORS?

For most games there is no segregation of supporters. If segregation needs to be enforced, then the terraces at both the South and East sides are allocated to away fans. The oval stock car track means that supporters using the end terrace are set rather far back from the action. For this reason, supporters tend to congregate on either side of the ground, where you are a bit closer to the pitch. As the perimeter wall surrounding the stadium is not that high, you can often see a few dotted faces, peering over it and watching the game for nothing!

WHERE TO DRINK

There is a small bar at the stadium itself, which is both popular with home and away supporters, plus there is also the nearby Park Bar which is also quite popular. Otherwise there are a number of other bars located on or around the nearby High St.

GETTING THERE & WHERE TO PARK

The ground is located in the centre of the town, beside the High Street; however, it is not easily visible when driving along the High Street itself.

Leave the M90 at Junction 3 and take the A92 towards Kirkcaldy. Then take the A909 into Cowdenbeath, which then leads into the High Street. After a short distance along the High Street, there is a small parking sign entitled 'Central Park' which points left down a small road for the ground. If you miss the sign (as I did), continue further up the High Street and turn left into Stenhouse Street where there is an overflow car park used on matchdays. There is also a fair sized car park at the ground as well, which is free to use.

By Train

Cowdenbeath station is only five minutes walk from the ground and is served by trains from Edinburgh.

LOCAL RIVALS

East Fife.

ADMISSION PRICES

Terrace: Adults £8. Concessions: £3.

Seating:

A £1 surcharge is paid within the ground to access the seating area.

PROGRAMME

Official Programme: £1.

RECORD ATTENDANCE

25,586 v Glasgow Rangers. League Cup Quarter Final, September 21st 1949.

AVERAGE ATTENDANCE

2003-2004: 306 (Division Three).

DID YOU KNOW?

The Club were originally nicknamed the Miners, as at one time there was a mining pit adjacent to the ground.

DUMBARTON

Ground Name: Strathclyde Homes Stadium
Capacity: 2,050 (all-seated)
Address: Castle Road, Dumbarton G82 1JJ
Telephone No: 01389-762-569
Fax No: 01389-762-629
Pitch Size: 105m x 68m
Club Nickname: The Sons
Home Kit Colours: Yellow & Black
Official Website:
www.dumbartonfootballclub.com
Unofficial Websites:
Sons Supporters Trust - www.sonstrust.net
Dumbarton Mad (Footy Mad Network) - www.dumbarton-ad.co.uk

WHAT'S THE GROUND LIKE?

The ground, opened in 2000, is situated spectacularly under the Castle Rock. It currently comprises of one stand which sits at one side of the pitch. However the stand is of a fair size, is covered and all seated. The space and height between rows is ample, giving fans a good view of the action. One unusual aspect of the ground is that the team dugouts are on the opposite side of the ground to the dressing rooms and this results in a large procession at half and full time. The ground was built by Barr Construction and there is plenty of space around the area, which could be used for future expansion. David Carson adds: 'Most fans refer to the ground name as being The Rock Stadium'.

WHAT'S IT LIKE FOR VISITORS?

Away fans are situated in sections one and two, at one end of the new stand. Around 500 fans can be accommodated in this area. As you would expect from a new stand, the facilities are good and you should experience a hassle free day at the ground.

WHERE TO DRINK

The nearest bar that I could find was in the Rock Bowling Club, which is just a little further down the road from the ground, opposite the entrance to the castle. Otherwise there is the Stag's Head, situated opposite the entrance to East Dumbarton station. It is a good sized bar, with TVs and pool tables, but unfortunately does not serve fans wearing football colours.

GETTING THERE & WHERE TO PARK

Castle Rock dominates the Dumbarton skyline, and with the ground sitting just beneath, it is fairly easy to find your bearings. Follow the A814 into Dumbarton and just after you go under a railway bridge, you will see a sign pointing left for Dumbarton Castle. Turn left here (Victoria Street) and the ground is down the bottom of this road on the right. There is a fair sized car park at the ground.

By Train

Dumbarton East station is only a five minute walk from the ground. As you come out of the station, turn right along the main street, left into Victoria Street and the ground is down the bottom of this road on the right.

LOCAL RIVALS

Greenock Morton.

ADMISSION PRICES

Adults: £10.
Concessions: £5.

PROGRAMME

Official Programme: £1.50

RECORD ATTENDANCE

At Strathclyde Homes Stadium:
1,959 v Queens Park,
Division Three, April 27th 2002.
At Boghead Park:
18,000 v Raith Rovers, 1957.

AVERAGE ATTENDANCE

2003-2004: 1,039 (Division Two).

DID YOU KNOW?

The Club played at their previous Boghead Park ground for 121 years. It was then Scotland's oldest Football League Ground.

EAST FIFE

Ground Name: Bayview Stadium
Capacity: 2,000 (all-seated)
Address: Harbour View, Methil, Fife KY8 3RW
Telephone No: 01333-426-323
Fax No: 01333-426-376
Pitch Size: 115 x 75 yards
Club Nickname: Fifers
Home Kit Colours: Black & Gold
Official Website: www.eastfife.org
Unofficial Websites:
East Fife History - http://members.tripod.com/~corstorphine/historian.html
East Fife Unofficial (Sport Network) - www.sportnetwork.net/index.php?sid=17
C'mon On The Fife - www.freewebs.com/effc/
Away From The Numbers - www.aftn.co.uk

WHAT'S THE GROUND LIKE?

The ground was opened in 1998 after the Club moved from its old Bayview ground. It currently has only one stand, which sits at one side of the pitch. However the stand is of a fair size, is covered and all-seated. The space and height between rows is adequate, giving fans a good view of the action.

WHAT'S IT LIKE FOR VISITORS?

Away fans are located in the North part of the Main Stand, where up to 1,000 can be accommodated. The facilities, as you would expect from a new ground, are good, with even the stadium music and announcer piped through to the toilets! The ground is right on the coast and at times a biting wind can come off the North Sea so make sure that you wrap up well. On the down side, though, I would have to say that the outlook from this stand over the back of the ground has to be one of the ugliest I have seen at a football ground, with some huge old power station sitting beyond the grounds' perimeter.

WHERE TO DRINK

There is a social club above the Main Stand, which welcomes away fans. It is quite a comfortable club, enjoying views across the ground.

GETTING THERE & WHERE TO PARK

The ground is quite easy to find as it is situated on the seafront and is quite visible from a distance. From Kirkcaldy take the A911 towards Methil and then the A915 to Leven. Then turn right onto the A955 towards Leven and Methil. Follow the A955 through Methil towards Buckhaven. As you go along the seafront, the ground should be visible over to your left. Turn left onto the B932 (South Street) and then left again into Harbour View Road. The ground is down the bottom of this road on the left. There is a fair sized car park at the ground.

By Train

There is no railway station in Methil itself. The nearest is in Kirkcaldy which is around eight miles away.

LOCAL RIVALS

Raith Rovers, Cowdenbeath.

ADMISSION PRICES

Adults: £10. Concessions: £5.

PROGRAMME

Official Programme: £1.

RECORD ATTENDANCE

At Bayview Stadium:
1,900 v Queens Park
Division Three, May 10th 2003.
At Bayview:
22,515 v Raith Rovers
Division One, January 2nd, 1950.

AVERAGE ATTENDANCE

2003-2004: 708 (Division Two).

DID YOU KNOW?

That East Fife is the only Second Division Club ever to win the Scottish FA Cup, which they did in 1938.

EAST STIRLINGSHIRE

Ground Name: Firs Park
Capacity: 1,880 (200 seated)
Address: Firs Street, Falkirk FK2 7AY
Telephone No: 01324 623-583
Fax No: 01324 637-862
Pitch Size: 112 x 72 yards
Club Nickname: The Shire
Home Kit Colours: Black & White Hoops
Official Website: None at present
Unofficial Websites:
East Stirlingshire Mad (Footy Mad Network) - www.eaststirlingshire-mad.co.uk
Unofficial East Stirlingshire - www.east-stirling.150m.com

WHAT'S THE GROUND LIKE?

The ground is largely open, being predominantly terracing. One side has a small covered main stand, which is full of charm. Although it only runs for only about one-third of the length of the pitch, it is of a classic design, seen at many other older grounds around the country. The seated area of this stand is elevated above the pitch, which means that spectators have to climb a set of steps to reach it. On the other side is a partly covered terrace, which unfortunately has a number of floodlight pylons running across the front of it. At one end is a larger open terrace, whilst the other end is not used. This area just has a concrete wall running the length of it, which does look somewhat out of place with the rest of the ground. As it is quite small, a number of footballs are kicked out of the ground during the game and this keeps representatives of the club fairly busy in retrieving them.

FUTURE DEVELOPMENTS

Kenneth Manson informs me: 'The Club have announced a plan to sell their ground in Falkirk to a property developer for £1.5 million and move to nearby Grangemouth. They would play at the Grangemouth Athletics Stadium and use half of the money from the sale of the ground to further redevelop it. As part of the plan, the Club will also rename themselves Grangemouth Football Club. However, no formal timescales have been announced as to when this might take place'.

WHAT'S IT LIKE FOR VISITORS?

Martin Hart, a visiting Raith supporter tells me: 'There is no segregation in place at Firs Park, unless I'd imagine 'Shire were playing against local rivals. The ground is very easy to find, situated at the back of the Central Retail Park, which is full of parking spaces, and within 5 minutes walk of Firs Park. Otherwise, there is limited street parking outside the ground. The nearby Central Retail Park contains a McDonald's restaurant, however inside the ground there is a fantastic selection of food on offer, and at very reasonable prices. The pies are wonderful and you can even buy homemade chicken pakora for £2. My overall verdict: A thoroughly enjoyable day out at Firs Park, which incidentally is a very tidy ground, although facilities are a little on the sparse side. Other than that, a big thumbs up to East Stirlingshire from me'.

WHERE TO DRINK

A short walk from the ground is Gordons Bar & Lounge, which is popular with both home and away fans.

GETTING THERE & WHERE TO PARK

Follow the A904 into Falkirk. After passing Middlefield Road on your right, take the next right into Thornhill Road and then left into Firs Street for the ground.
Remember also to ignore the 'football traffic' signs around the area, as if you follow them you will eventually end up at Falkirk's ground. Street parking.

By Train

The nearest station is Grahamston which is about a 10 minute walk away from the ground. As you come out of the station, go left up Grahams Road and then turn right at the roundabout. Proceed through the retail park, before turning left into Victoria Road. The ground is down at the bottom of this road.

Thanks to Ben Smith for providing the directions.

LOCAL RIVALS

Falkirk, Stenhousemuir.

ADMISSION PRICES

All areas of the ground:
Adults: £8. Concessions; £4.

PROGRAMME

Official Programme: 50p.

RECORD ATTENDANCE

12,000 v Partick Thistle
Scottish Cup, 3rd Round, February 21st 1921.

AVERAGE ATTENDANCE

2003-2004: 278 (Division Three).

DID YOU KNOW?

The Club renamed itself from Bainsford Britannia to East Stirlingshire in 1881. It was the same name as a local cricket club, whose ground they took over.

ELGIN CITY

Ground Name: Borough Briggs
Capacity: 3,927 (478 seated)
Address: Borough Briggs Road, Elgin IV30 1AP
Telephone No: 01343-551-114
Fax No: 01343-547-921
Pitch Size: 110 x 75 yards
Club Nickname: Black & Whites
Home Kit Colours: Black & White Stripes
Official Website: None at present
Unofficial Website:
Elgincity.com - www.elgincity.com

WHAT'S THE GROUND LIKE?

On one side of the ground is a small, covered Main Stand. This all-seater stand runs for only about half the length of the pitch and straddles the halfway line. There is terracing to one side of this stand. On the other side of the ground is a small covered terrace, which is divided between home and away supporters. This enclosure looks quite old and has a number of supporting pillars. Both ends have new-ish open terraces that are set back from the pitch. These were opened in the year 2000. An unusual aspect of the ground is the odd looking floodlights running down each side of the pitch, the bases of which, on the enclosure side, go down through the roof and onto the terrace, further hindering the spectators' view of the action.

WHAT'S IT LIKE FOR VISITORS?

Away fans are located on the Western side of the covered enclosure. This stand is a little grim and the views of the action, unless you are right in the front of the stand, can be quite poor as there are a number of supporting pillars to contend with. The facilities in this area are fairly basic, but at least it is covered and even a small number of away fans can really make some noise from this terrace. You will normally find a warm welcome at Borough

Briggs and this makes for a good day out.

WHERE TO DRINK

There is a supporters' social club which welcomes away fans, the entrance to which is located behind the Main Stand. The social club is quite comfortable, so much so that the barman was telling me that on one occasion, two supporters from Stranraer never left the bar all Saturday afternoon and didn't get to see the game!

GETTING THERE & WHERE TO PARK

Coming from the East or West along the A96, continue into Elgin until you reach the roundabout which has Elgin Town Hall situated on one corner. Turn at this roundabout onto the A941 (North Street) towards Lossiemouth. After a short distance down this road, take the second road on your left (Borough Briggs Road) and the ground is situated down this on your right. There is plenty of street parking around the ground.

By Train
Elgin train station is about a mile from the ground and should take about 15 minutes to walk. Kevin Craig provides the following directions: 'As you leave the station, turn left and continue up a steep hill. Continue straight on this road crossing two roundabouts and at the third roundabout turn left. Go up this road for some 500 yards and you will see the ground on your left hand side'.

LOCAL RIVALS

Peterhead, Inverness Caledonian Thistle, Lossiemouth and Forres.

ADMISSION PRICES

Seating: Adults £8. Concessions £5.
Terrace: Adults £6. Concessions £3.

PROGRAMME

Official Programme: £1.

RECORD ATTENDANCE

12,608 v Arbroath
Scottish Cup, February 17th, 1968.

AVERAGE ATTENDANCE

2003-2004: 526 (Division Three).

DID YOU KNOW?

The Club have played at Borough Briggs since 1921. At one time the ground was overlooked by an old World War Two concrete pillbox. This was demolished to make way for a new terrace in the year 2000.

FALKIRK

Ground Name: Falkirk Stadium
Capacity: 4,200 (all-seated)
Address: Westfield, Falkirk FK2 9DX
Telephone No: 01324-624-121
Fax No: 01324-612-418
Pitch Size: 110 x 72 yards
Club Nickname: Bairns
Home Kit Colours: Navy Blue, White & Red
Official Website: www.falkirkfc.co.uk
Unofficial Websites:
It's Been Chalked Off - www.thebairninholland.com
Falkirk Mad (Footy Mad Network) - www.falkirk-mad.co.uk

WHAT'S THE GROUND LIKE?

After leaving their old Brockville Ground in 2003, home since 1876, and then ground sharing with Stenhousemuir for one season, the Club have now taken up residence on the very outskirts of Falkirk. Named the Falkirk Stadium, it currently only comprises one stand, at one side of the stadium. But what a stand it is! A huge cantilever affair that houses 4,200 supporters, it looks spectacular both close up and from a distance. In terms of design, it is probably one of the best new stands constructed in Britain for some years. It is two-tiered, with a large lower tier and a small upper tier with comparatively small windshields to either side.

FUTURE GROUND DEVELOPMENTS

Kevin Dunn informs me: 'The Club intend to build a second stand at the North End of the stadium. It is planned to house 2,200 fans and is scheduled to be completed by the end of 2004. There are then plans to build a South Stand, which will be virtually identical to the North Stand and then an East Stand, which will house a further 4,200 fans. However, these latter two proposals are dependant on the Club securing the necessary finance. If completed, the overall capacity will rise to 12,800.

WHAT'S IT LIKE FOR VISITORS?

I have yet to visit the stadium to watch a game, but would expect from such a new stand that the facilities will be good and that you will have a good view of the playing action.

WHERE TO DRINK

Being on the outskirts of Falkirk there are few bars or even a handy chippy nearby. Probably best to drink somewhere on the way beforehand or else take the 20-25 minute walk into Falkirk town centre where there are plenty of bars to be found. Kevin Dunn adds: 'There is a bar called Pennies at the old ice rink, just off the Grangemouth Road. Go up Grangemouth Road towards the town centre and you will pass the college and the old ice rink (which is now an indoor football centre) on the left hand side. The pub is just down the right hand side of the old ice rink, near to the Saturday market'.

GETTING THERE & WHERE TO PARK

From The East:
Leave the M9 at Junction 5 and take the A9 towards Falkirk. After about a mile, you will be able to see the stadium over on your right.
From The West:
Leave the M9 at Junction 6 and take the A904 towards Falkirk. You will reach the stadium on your left.
At the time of writing there are no details of parking facilities at the stadium; however there looked to be a fair amount of street parking available in a residential area across the road from it.

By Train
Falkirk Grahamston Station is about a mile away from the stadium. It is a fairly straight 20 minute walk down the A904 Grangemouth Road. As you come out of the station, turn left and follow the ring road round (A803) to the right. Turn left into Weir Street and at the bottom of the street turn left onto Kerse Lane. This is the A904 which leads into Ladysmill and then becomes Grangemouth Road. Go straight down this road and you will eventually reach the stadium over on your right.

LOCAL RIVALS

St Johnstone and Dunfermline.

ADMISSION PRICES

West Stand (Centre): Adults £18, no concessions.
West Stand (Wings): Adults £15. Concessions: £10. Under 12s £5. Adult and under 12s: £18, each additional under 12 £3.

PROGRAMME

Official Programme: £2.

RECORD ATTENDANCE

At Brockville:
23,100 v Celtic, February 21st, 1953.

AVERAGE ATTENDANCE

2003-2004: 2,631 (Division One).

DID YOU KNOW?

The Club's nickname "Bairns" comes from the motto of the old Burgh of Falkirk - 'Better meddle wi' the deil than the Bairns O' Falkirk'.

FORFAR ATHLETIC

Ground Name: Station Park
Capacity: 4,602 (seated 739)
Address: Carseview Road, Forfar, Angus DD8 3BT
Telephone No: 01307-463-576
Fax No: 01307-466-956
Pitch Size: 115 x 69 yards
Club Nickname: Loons
Home Kit Colours: Sky Blue & Navy Blue

Official Website:
www.forfarathletic.co.uk

Unofficial Websites:
The Loonatic - www.theloonatic.co.uk
Loons Mad (Footy Mad Network) - www.loons-mad.co.uk

WHAT'S THE GROUND LIKE?

The ground is predominantly terracing, with terraces behind each goal and along one side of the pitch. The terraces at each end of the ground are not covered and are open to the elements. At one end is the small East Terrace, whilst opposite is the larger West Terrace. The latter is unusual in being taller on one side than the other. On one side of the ground is the Main Stand, which is a traditional looking covered, seated stand. The seating is raised above pitch level and there are a number of supporting pillars at its front. This stand only runs for around half the length of the pitch. The team dugouts are located in front of this stand. On the other side is a small covered terrace that runs the full length of the pitch. This stand looks relatively new and has a number of small floodlights protruding from its roof. There is quite a slope to the pitch that runs down across the ground from the West Terrace down to the East Terrace.

WHAT'S IT LIKE FOR VISITORS?

Normally segregation of supporters is not in force, so most away fans tend to head for the covered South Terrace. If segregation takes place, then the open West Terrace is allocated to away supporters plus part of the Main Stand.

The facilities are fairly basic around the ground, but as you would expect the bridies are pretty good!

WHERE TO DRINK

Dave Mair informs me that the nearest bar is located at the Commercial Hotel, which is a five minute walk away from the ground. There are also a number of bakeries selling more of the legendary Forfar Bridies.

GETTING THERE & WHERE TO PARK

The ground is located right on the outskirts of town. In fact, the Main Stand backs onto fields. From the A90 take the A926 towards Forfar. At the T Junction, turn right into Brechin Road, then turn left into Market Street and then second left into Carseview Road for the ground. There is only limited parking available at the ground; otherwise there is the nearby Muir Street car park or street parking.

By Train

Even though the ground is called Station Park, there is in fact no railway station in Forfar itself. The nearest stations are in Dundee or Arbroath, both around 14 miles away!

LOCAL RIVALS

Brechin, Arbroath and Montrose.

ADMISSION PRICES

Seating: Adults £9.50. Concessions £4.50.
Terrace: Adults £9. Concessions £4.50.

PROGRAMME

Official Programme: £1.

RECORD ATTENDANCE

10,780 v Glasgow Rangers
Scottish Cup 2nd Round, Feb. 2nd, 1970.

AVERAGE ATTENDANCE

2003-2004: 663 (Division Two).

DID YOU KNOW?

The Club's nickname "Loons" is derived from the local dialect 'Loon' which means a 'strapping young man' usually connected with agriculture.

GRETNA

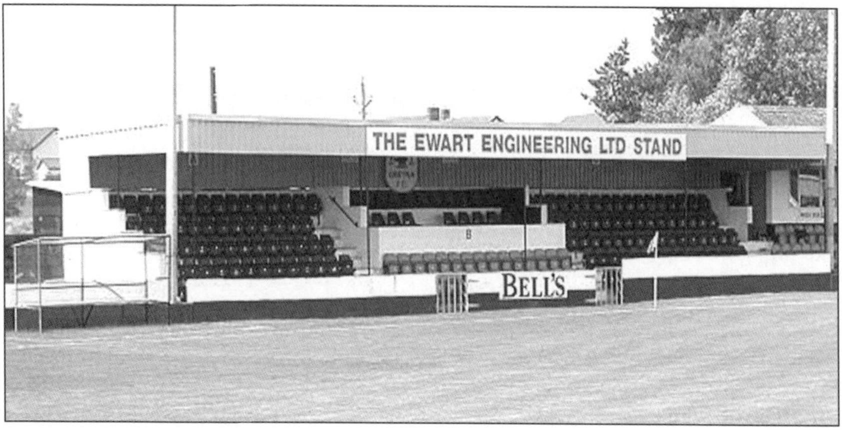

Ground Name: Raydale Park
Capacity: 2,200
Address: Dominion Road, Gretna DG16 5AP
Telephone No: 01461-337-602
Fax No: 01461-338-047
Pitch Size: 105 x 68m
Club Nickname: Black & Whites or Borderers
Home Kit Colours: Black & White
Official Website: www.gretnafootballclub.co.uk
Unofficial Website: Gretna Mad (Footy Mad Network) - www.gretna-mad.co.uk

WHAT'S THE GROUND LIKE?

The ground is on the small side and is predominantly terracing, with three sides being largely for standing supporters. Each of these areas is quite small, being only a few feet deep. One end, known as the "Long Stand", is a simple covered terrace which is for home supporters. This has a number of small supporting pillars running across the front of it and four white flag poles on its roof. Opposite is a small open terrace, which is allocated to away fans. On one side is the Ewart Engineering (Main) Stand, which is a small covered, all-seated stand. Opposite is another simple covered area, which on one side is terrace and on the other there are just two rows of seating. Again there is a row of supporting pillars along the entire length of the stand. There is a Club Shop located inside the ground on the Main Stand side of the ground. The ground is pleasantly well situated with lots of trees surrounding it, although the newish looking set of floodlights (four running down each side of the ground), do little to enhance it.

WHAT'S IT LIKE FOR VISITORS?

The League's relative newcomers offer a pleasant and hassle free day out, although the portaloos available in the away end leave a lot to be desired. Peter Llewellyn adds: 'Make sure to try the pies as they are excellent'.

WHERE TO DRINK

There is a supporters' Club House at the edge of the car park, which allows in away supporters.

GETTING THERE & WHERE TO PARK

From the M74 take the B7076 towards Gretna, then turn onto the B721 which will take you through Gretna itself. After crossing Central Avenue (which has a few shops along it), take the third left into Dominion Road for the ground. There is a sign at the end of Dominion Road pointing in the direction of the Club and Sunday market. There is a large car park adjacent to the ground which costs £1.00.

By Train

The ground is around a 15 minute walk away from Gretna Green station.

LOCAL RIVALS

Queen Of The South and Annan Athletic.

ADMISSION PRICES

Seating:

Adults £8. Concessions £4.

Terrace:

Adults £7. Concessions £3.50.

PROGRAMME

Official Programme: £1.50.

RECORD ATTENDANCE

2,307 v Rochdale
FA Cup 1st Round, November 16th 1991.

AVERAGE ATTENDANCE

2003-2004: 465 (Division Three).

DID YOU KNOW?

That from its formation in 1946 until the 2002/03 season, the Club used to compete in English non-League football.

HAMILTON ACADEMICAL

Ground Name: New Douglas Park
Capacity: 5,300 (all-seated)
Address: Cadzow Avenue, Hamilton, Lanarkshire ML3 0FT
Telephone No: 01698-368-650
Fax No: 01698-285-422
Pitch Size: 115 x 75 yards
Club Nickname: The Accies
Home Kit Colours: Red & White
Official Website: None at present
Unofficial Website:
Accies World - www.acciesworld.com

WHAT'S THE GROUND LIKE?

At long last the Club have their own home, after spending seven years of ground sharing with other clubs, since giving up their Douglas Park ground in 1994. The new ground, which is near to the former site of the original Douglas Park (now a Sainsburys Supermarket), was opened in time for the 2001/02 season and even though it currently has only two sides, it is at least somewhere the fans can call home, once again. Both stands are covered all-seated stands at one side and at one end of the pitch. They are unusual, in terms of modern stands, in that they are both raised above pitch level, which means that spectators have to climb a set of stairs to reach the seated area. There are also four striking floodlight pylons in each corner of the ground.

WHAT'S IT LIKE FOR VISITORS?

Away fans are normally housed in one section of the Main Stand, where the view of the action is good. For clubs with a larger following, the North Stand will be allocated instead. Alan Redman, a visiting Morton supporter, adds: 'There is plenty of legroom in the North Stand, but wrap up well in winter because the ground is largely open, the wind blows right through it'.

Ross Clark, a Hamilton fan, tells me: 'Despite having only the two stands at the moment, it's possible to make quite a lot of noise from either stand. You kind of forget that there's nothing on the other side of the pitch until the ball goes out and it takes the ball boys far too long to retrieve it from the far wall (a few impatient staff have taken to just punting a new one on almost as soon as it happens). The evening matches have been better for atmosphere'.

WHERE TO DRINK

There is a Social Club in the Main Stand where away fans are welcome. Whilst Craig Irvine recommends The Clansman Bar in nearby Burnbank, which is a decent pub. There are two other local bars at Peacock Cross: the Silver Tassie and Harvies. The Chambers at the court is also not bad.

GETTING THERE & WHERE TO PARK

Leave the M74 at Junction 5, and follow the signs for Hamilton. You will pass the racecourse on your left and a large fire station on your right. At the first set of traffic lights, turn right into Caird Street. On your left will appear a fair sized car park, where you can park and walk 10 minutes to the ground. Or if you continue along Caird Street, turn right just before the traffic lights (and bingo hall) into New Park Street and you will come to the ground entrance on your left. There is a reasonable sized car park there which costs £2.00.

By Train

The ground is only a few minutes walk from Hamilton West station, which is served by trains from Glasgow Central. Please note that Hamilton Central station is quite far away from the ground.

LOCAL RIVALS

Motherwell.

ADMISSION PRICES

Adults: £10. Concessions: £5.

PROGRAMME

Official Programme: £2.

RECORD ATTENDANCE

At New Douglas Park:
4,280 v Sunderland (Friendly Match Played In 2001).
At Douglas Park:
28,690 v Hearts (1937).

AVERAGE ATTENDANCE

2003-2004: 1,403 (Division Two).

DID YOU KNOW?

The Club got its name from the local Hamilton Academy school.

INVERNESS CALEDONIAN THISTLE

Ground Name: Caledonian Stadium
Capacity: 6,500 (seated 2,200)
Address: East Longman, Inverness IV1 1FF
Telephone No: 01463-222-880
Fax No: 01463-715-816
Pitch Size: 115 x 75 yards
Club Nickname: Caley Thistle
Home Kit Colours: Royal Blue, Red & White

Official Website:
Caley Thistle Online (Sport Network) - www.sportnetwork.net/main/s14.php

Unofficial Websites:
Caley Nostalgia - www.caledonianfc.co.uk
Write On Caley - http://writeoncaley.tripod.com
Caley Jags - www.caleyjags.com

WHAT'S THE GROUND LIKE?

The ground is dominated by the Main Stand at one side of the pitch. This all-seated stand is quite smart looking and is partly covered (to the rear), whilst opposite is a small open terrace. At one end, the Bridge End Terrace has recently been covered and is the 'home end' of the ground. Richard Laird adds: 'The North Terrace (Bridge End) has been renamed The Kevin Bisset Enclosure after a local referee whose career was cut short because of illness". The other end, the South Terrace, is another small open terrace that is given to away supporters. Each of these terraces is set well back from the pitch. One unusual fact about the Caledonian stadium is that it has the widest pitch of any league team in Scotland.

The Club was formed in 1994, following a merger of two clubs: Inverness Thistle and Caledonian FC. The new club were admitted to the Scottish League for the 1994-95 season.

WHAT'S IT LIKE FOR VISITORS?

Away supporters are housed mainly in the South Terrace at one end of the ground. A number of seats are also made available in the South part of the Main Stand. As these areas are mostly uncovered, pray it doesn't rain. Coupled with the fact that the ground is built right on the coast of the Moray Firth means that there can be some biting cold winds coming off the sea. Still the ground has quite a picturesque setting and from the away end you get a grand view of the Moray Firth Bridge climbing up into the distance.

WHERE TO DRINK

John Blair informs me: 'There are no pubs as yet around the ground. There is one due to be opened at the ground, but at the moment the nearest pubs are about half a mile away towards town centre. In town there are plenty of good pubs. Try the Gellions, the Phoenix, Gunsmiths, or the Caley Club (near Caledonian FC's old ground) which has plenty of history. Most home fans tend to head for The Innes Bar on Innes Street near the harbour. It's about a 20 minute walk from the stadium'.

GETTING THERE & WHERE TO PARK

By car
The ground is straightforward to find and depending on which approach you take into Inverness, the bright orange cantilevers of the Main Stand can be seen for quite some distance away. Continue on the A9 through Inverness and at the roundabout, just before the large bridge across the Moray Firth, turn right for the road down to the ground. There are a couple of good sized car parks (£1) at each end of the ground.
By Train
Inverness station is just under a mile away from the ground, which is about a 15-20 minute walk. However, there is a free bus service from Inverness bus station (Farraline Park).

LOCAL RIVALS

Ross County.

ADMISSION PRICES

Seating:
Adults: £11. Concessions*: £6.
Terracing:
Adults: £9. Concessions*: £3.
*Concessions apply to under 16s, OAPs, the unemployed and students.

PROGRAMME

Official Programme: £1.50.

RECORD ATTENDANCE

6,290 v Aberdeen.
February 20th, 2000, Tennents Scottish Cup 4th Round.

AVERAGE ATTENDANCE

2003-2004: 2,375 (Division One).

DID YOU KNOW?

With 26 letters, the Club have the longest name in Scottish and English League football.

Please note that at the time of going to print it was still unclear as to which division Inverness will be playing in for the 2004/05 season or in fact which ground they will be playing at. At the time of writing First Division Champions Inverness are currently appealing against a decision not to admit them to the SPL (their ground currently does not meet SPL criteria). If their appeal is upheld then they may ground share with Aberdeen (even though it is over 100 miles away) or be given special dispensation to continue playing at the Caledonian Stadium. If the appeal is overturned then Inverness will remain in Division One.

MONTROSE

Ground Name: Links Park
Capacity: 3,292 (1,338 seated)
Address: Wellington St, Montrose DD10 8QD
Telephone No: 01674-673-200
Fax No: 01674-677-311
Pitch Size: 113 x 70 yards
Club Nickname: The Gable Endies
Home Kit Colours: Royal Blue & White
Official Website:
www.montrosefc.co.uk
Unofficial Websites:
Mo Mo Super Mo (Sport Network) - www.sportnetwork.net/main/s162.htm
Montrose Mad (Footy Mad Network) - www.montrose-mad.co.uk

WHAT'S THE GROUND LIKE?

The ground is largely open, with one side unused for spectators and one end being a small open terrace, comprising of just six rows. The Main Stand is a single-tiered covered stand, which is all-seated with just over 1,300 seats. It has a cantilever roof, meaning that there are no supporting pillars to obstruct your view. This stand only runs for around half the length of the pitch and straddles the halfway line. The Wellington Street End is a small covered terrace that is a strange looking affair. It is set well back from the pitch, does not run the full width of it and on one side the covered terrace kinks around towards the pitch itself, but not around the corner flag as you would expect. Whether this was designed to help protect the fans against the prevailing wind I don't know, but it certainly looks odd. There is also a row of supporting pillars at this end, plus a small fence that runs across the front of it. The ground is completed with a set of four modern looking floodlight pylons, one in each corner.

WHAT'S IT LIKE FOR VISITORS?

Normally segregation is not in force at Links Park. However, if it is enforced, then half the Main Stand (around 700 seats) is allocated, with away fans also being allowed to stand around the perimeter of the ground, on the two sides that are not in use. Links Park is normally a good day out and the pies are great, but at times the ground lacks a little in atmosphere.

Jon Blackwood adds: 'Links Park rarely sees crowds of more than 500 these days, although Montrose could count on 800-1000 in their days in the first division. Pre-season friendlies against Aberdeen and Dundee United, and derby games against Arbroath, always attract four figure crowds. Other than the odd lively atmosphere for derby games against Montrose's bitter rivals, Arbroath, there is never, ever any trouble and the home fans are friendly. There's not a huge amount to do in Montrose but if it's a sunny early or end of season game, the beach is great and it's worth looking at the distinctive Auld Kirk building'.

WHERE TO DRINK

Douglas Walker informs me: 'The nearest bar is the Golf Inn on Mill Street. It is only a five minute walk away from the ground'. John Laidlaw adds: 'There is a British Legion Club near the turnstiles, which from a distance looks more like a house rather than a Club (there is a small yellow sign attached to a wall above the entrance). It will sometimes allow non-members to be signed in, which is worth the effort as it serves a cracking pint'. Otherwise if you are walking from the train station then the Corner House Hotel next to the Auld Kirk is worth a visit.

GETTING THERE & WHERE TO PARK

The ground is signposted from the A92, as you enter the town.

From The North:
Take the A92 into Montrose. Just as the road turns towards the seafront, turn left into Rosehill Road. Take the fourth right into Warrack Terrace and then third left into Wellington Street for the ground.

From The South:
Take the A92 to the outskirts of Montrose. Turn right into Wharf Street (B9133 signposted football traffic) and then bear left into Hill Street. Continue straight on up this road going over a crossroads into Panmore Place (signposted Sports Centre). Follow this road passing the Town Hall on your right and then as you run alongside a small strip of park on your right, you should be able to see the floodlights of the ground just beyond it. Turn right into Wellington Street for the ground.

There is a fair sized car park at the ground, otherwise street parking.

By Train
Montrose railway station is approximately one mile away from Links Park and should take be around a 15 minutes walk. From the train station, cross over the Somerfield Car park and head towards the spire of the Auld Kirk. Turn left onto Hume Street, then left again onto the High Street. Cross the road, then right down John Street. Keep straight ahead, crossing over Mill Street and Provost Scott Road. Turn left up Eastern Road, then right when you come to Wellington Street. You'll see the home turnstiles straight ahead of you. Otherwise a taxi from the station to the ground should cost about £3. Thanks to Jon Blackwood for providing the above directions.

LOCAL RIVALS

Arbroath, Forfar and Brechin City.

ADMISSION PRICES

Seating:
Adults: £7.50. Concessions £4.
Terrace:
Adults: £7. Concessions £3.50.

PROGRAMME

Official Programme: £1.50.

RECORD ATTENDANCE

8,983 v Dundee, Scottish Cup 3rd Round March 17th, 1973.

AVERAGE ATTENDANCE

2003-2004: 361 (Division Three).

DID YOU KNOW?

The Club's nickname of Gable Endies has its origins in the local architecture of Montrose, where many buildings have the gable end exposed onto the street.

MORTON

Ground Name: Cappielow Park
Capacity: 11,100 (seated 5,741)
Address: Sinclair Street, Greenock PA15 2TY
Telephone No: 01475 723-571
Fax No: 01475 781-084
Pitch Size: 110 x 71 yards
Club Nickname: Ton
Home Kit Colours: Royal Blue & White
Official Website: www.gmfc.net
Unofficial Websites:
Morton Unofficial - www.mortonunofficial.net
Supporters Trust - www.gmst.org.uk
Greenock Morton Supporters Online - www.go.to/greenockmorton

WHAT'S THE GROUND LIKE?

Cappielow is a fair sized ground, full of character, but beginning to show its age. However, with a new Chairman on board, efforts are being made to brighten up and improve the overall state of the ground. The Grandstand, on one side of the ground, is a single-tiered, all-seated stand, which has a number of supporting pillars in front. On its roof are a set of unusual striking floodlights, another set of which are also on the stand opposite. The Cowshed, as it is known, is a classic looking stand and is unusual in that it has seating at the front of it and terracing at its rear. Both ends are open to the elements. The Wee Dublin End is a former terrace with white benches bolted onto it, which makes it look out of place. This end is normally not used on match days. Beyond can be seen a large crane, which is reminiscent of the ship building days on the Clyde. Opposite is the small Sinclair Street Terrace which has a small clock behind it.

WHAT'S IT LIKE FOR VISITORS?

Fans are housed in one side of the Grandstand, towards the Dublin End of the ground. There are a fair few pillars in this stand that may impede your view and the legroom is on the tight side. For larger games then the Wee Dublin End can also be allocated for away fans to use. A visit to Cappielow is normally a relaxed day out and the Morton fans do their best to get behind their team.

WHERE TO DRINK

The Norseman Bar is right by the ground and is popular with both home and away fans. It can get quite busy on matchdays, but it is still the favoured pre-match venue.

GETTING THERE & WHERE TO PARK

From Glasgow take the M8 and then A8 towards Greenock (along which you get a fine view of Castle Rock in Dumbarton). Follow the A8 into Greenock and you will reach the ground on your left which is just after going under a bridge with Picollo's fish & chips shop on the corner. There is a car park opposite the main entrance, otherwise street parking.

By Train

The nearest station to the ground is Cartsdyke which lies on the Glasgow Central - Gourock line. The journey from Glasgow takes around 40 minutes and then the ground is only five minutes walk from the station.

LOCAL RIVALS

St Mirren and Dumbarton.

ADMISSION PRICES

Seating:

Adults: £11. Concessions: £6. Adult + 1 Child: £14.

Terrace:

Adults: £9. Concessions: £5. Under 15s: £2. Adult + 1 Child: £11.

PROGRAMME

Official Programme: £1.50.

RECORD ATTENDANCE

23,500 v Celtic
April 29th, 1922.

AVERAGE ATTENDANCE

2003-2004: 2,945 (Division Two).

DID YOU KNOW?

The Club got its name from the street where a number of its original founders lived - Morton Terrace.

PETERHEAD

Ground Name: Balmoor Stadium
Capacity: 4,000 (seated 998)
Address: Lord Catto Park, Peterhead AB42 1EU
Telephone No: 01779-478-256
Fax No: 01779-490-682
Pitch Size: 105 x 70 yards
Club Nickname: The Blue Toon
Home Kit Colours: Blue & White
Official Website:
www.peterheadfc.org.uk
Unofficial Website:
None at present

WHAT'S THE GROUND LIKE?

Balmoor has two virtually identical stands that run down each side of the ground. Both are all-seated, roughly of the same height and are covered. The seating areas are raised above pitch level, which means that supporters need to climb a small set of stairs at the front of the stand to access them. The West Stand has windshields at either side of it. Both ends of the ground are open and don't have any formal terracing.

Peterhead joined the Scottish Football League at the beginning of the 2000/2001 season. One of the reasons why they were invited to join was because of their move to the Balmoor Stadium, which was opened in 1997. Previously the Club played at Recreation Park, which was sold for redevelopment to Safeways.

WHAT'S IT LIKE FOR VISITORS?

David Gray informs me: 'The Balmoor Stadium is a friendly place where away fans are always made welcome. There is no segregation, so opposing fans are always able to mix with each other'. However, remember to wrap up well as the ground itself is quite exposed and there is often a cold biting wind coming off the North Sea.

WHERE TO DRINK

There is a Social Club located in the rear of the Main Stand which welcomes away supporters. Otherwise there are plenty of bars to be found in the centre of town, which is a 10 minute walk away.

GETTING THERE & WHERE TO PARK

The ground is located just out of town on the A982 Peterhead to Fraserburgh Road.

From The South:
From the A90 you can take the first exit for Peterhead (the A982). This will take you to the town centre where you continue following the A982 towards Fraserburgh. You will go past a swimming pool and will reach the ground on your left. There are around 200 car parking spaces at the ground which are free.

By Train
The nearest railway station is in Aberdeen, which is some 32 miles away! Therefore this ground has the record of being furthest from a station than any other League team in Britain.

LOCAL RIVALS

Elgin City and Fraserburgh.

ADMISSION PRICES

Adults: £7. Concessions: £3.

PROGRAMME

Official Programme: £1.50.

RECORD ATTENDANCE

At Recreation Park:
8,643 v Raith Rovers, 1987.
At Balmoor Stadium:
2,158 v Aberdeen, Friendly July 22nd 2003.

AVERAGE ATTENDANCE

2003-2004: 579 (Division Three).

DID YOU KNOW?

The Club played at their previous ground, Recreation Park, for 106 years before moving to Balmoor Stadium in 1997.

QUEEN OF THE SOUTH

Ground Name: Palmerston Park
Capacity: 6,412 (3,509 seated)
Address: Dumfries, DG2 9BA
Telephone No: 01387-254-853
Fax No: 01387-240-470
Pitch Size: 112 x 73 yards
Club Nickname: Doonhamers
Home Kit Colours: Royal Blue & White
Official Website: www.qosfc.com
Unofficial Websites:
Only One Team In The Bible - www.qosfan.co.uk
Queen Of The South Mad (Footy Mad Network) - www.queenofthesouth-mad.co.uk

WHAT'S THE GROUND LIKE?

Palmerston Park is a great looking traditional ground with a nice blend of new and old stands. On one side of the ground is the relatively new Galloway News (East) Stand. This smart looking, all-seated single-tier stand is covered and runs the full length of the pitch. Opposite is the Dumfries and Galloway Grandstand, a classic looking small covered seated stand which is raised. It only runs for around half the length of the pitch, straddling the halfway line. There are small portions of terracing at the front of the stand and at either side. At one end is the Portland Drive Terrace. This is a fair sized terrace that is partly covered (to the rear). The roof has a gable perched upon it, which features a traditional looking clock. The only downside to the stadium is the Terregles Street End, a small open terrace no longer used which has fallen into disrepair. The ground also has a striking set of floodlights.

WHAT'S IT LIKE FOR VISITORS?

Away fans are located in the relatively new Galloway News (East) Stand, which is shared with home supporters. Around half this stand is allocated, which is about 1,100 seats. If demand requires it, then the whole stand can be allocated, taking the total seats to 2,200. The facilities in this stand and view of the action are pretty good and even a small amount of away supporters can really generate some noise from it.

R. Shields, a visiting Clyde supporter, adds: 'This is perhaps one of the best, if not the best, day out in the first division. A hospitable ground, good facilities, placed in a town that is enjoyable to visit. Queens are good competition, and if I had to single out a favourite away game, then this would be it!'

WHERE TO DRINK

There is a bar at the ground at the rear of the West Stand called the Palmerston Lounge Bar where away fans are welcome. The nearest bar is the Spread Eagle Inn, which is about a five minute walk away. Around the corner from this bar, are a number of others including the Devorgilla and the Globe.

GETTING THERE & WHERE TO PARK

Approaching Dumfries from the North or East you will reach the A75 Dumfries bypass. Follow the signs for Kilmarnock/Stranraer and when you reach the roundabout that is the junction with the A76 (Glasgow Street), turn left towards Dumfries. Go over a couple of roundabouts and when you reach a T-junction with a set of traffic lights (you'll see the Spread Eagle Inn), turn right at the lights onto the A780. A short way down this road, turn right into Terregles Street for the ground. There is a fair amount of parking at the 'Ice Bowl' behind the Galloway News (East Stand), otherwise there is some street parking available.

By Train

Dumfries is served by trains from Glasgow and Carlisle. The ground is just over a mile from the ground and should take about 15-20 minutes to walk. When you arrive by train, you will see an imposing hotel right in front of you and behind it is a street called Lovers Walk. Turn right along Lovers Walk until you reach Academy Street. Continue along Academy Street bearing right past Burns Statue on to Buccleuch Street. Continue until you pass over Buccleuch Street Bridge then on to Galloway Street. Continue then turn right on to Terregles Street and about 200 yards further on is Palmerston Park. Thanks to Eric Fisher, for providing the directions.

LOCAL RIVALS

Stranraer.

ADMISSION PRICES

The Dumfries and Galloway Standard Stands:
Adults: £12. No concessions.
All other areas of the ground:
Adults: £10. Concessions: £6.

PROGRAMME

Official Programme: £1.50.

RECORD ATTENDANCE

26,552 v Hearts
Scottish Cup 3rd Round, February 23rd, 1952.

AVERAGE ATTENDANCE

2003-2004: 2,360 (Division One).

DID YOU KNOW?

The Club's nickname 'Doonhamers' comes from the local Dumfries saying 'Doon Hame' meaning 'Down Home'. 'Doonhamers' is therefore used to describe someone from Dumfries.

QUEENS PARK

Ground Name: Hampden Park
Capacity: 52,500 (all-seated)
Address: Mount Florida, Glasgow G42 9BA
Telephone No: 0141-632-1275
Fax No: 0141-636-1612
Pitch Size: 115 x 75 yards
Club Nickname: Spiders
Home Kit Colours: Black & White
Official Website:
www.queensparkfc.co.uk
Unofficial Website:
Queen's Park Fansite - www.queensparkfansite.cjb.net

WHAT'S THE GROUND LIKE?

The stadium has been completely redeveloped in recent years and the predominantly old terraced ground has now been transformed into a modern all-seated stadium. Although not particularly large for a national stadium, it still retains its charm and individual character which is enhanced by its completely enclosed oval shape. Three sides of the stadium are single-tiered, but the South Stand on one side of it has a small second tier, which slightly overhangs the lower one. Normally this might give the stadium an unbalanced look, but it has been well integrated with the rest of the stadium with its oval roof rising gently towards this stand. There are also two electric scoreboards suspended underneath the roofs at either end of the stadium. One unusual aspect of the stadium is that the team dugouts are actually situated six rows up on the South Stand. This is to allow team managers to get a better view of the game.

WHAT'S IT LIKE FOR VISITORS?

Only the BT Scotland South Stand is open for Queens Park games. It has some great facilities on the concourse, in the back of the stand. The legroom and view of the playing action are also good. Although a pleasant afternoon out, crowds of around the 1,000 mark, in a 52,500 seater stadium, does little for the atmosphere.

WHERE TO DRINK

There is the Queens Park Social Club, in Somerville Drive, which allows in away fans. Otherwise there are a number of bars and chippies around the stadium. My favourite is the Clockwork Beer Company on Cathcart Road (going away from the city centre). This spacious pub brews its own beers and stocks a wide range of whiskies.

GETTING THERE & WHERE TO PARK

Leave the M74 at Junction 1 and turn left at the roundabout into Fullarton Road, following the signs for Rutherglen. Go straight across the next roundabout and at the following roundabout turn right into Cambuslang Road. You will cross over the River Clyde and then continue to the end of this road. At the traffic lights turn right and continue along Main Street Rutherglen and then on towards Mount Florida. Continue straight along this road until you reach the large Asda Store at which you turn left into Aikenhead Road. The stadium is up this road on the right-hand side. There is a large free car park behind the South Stand.

By Train

The nearest stations to the stadium are Mount Florida and Kings Park. Both are served by trains from Glasgow Central (journey time around 10-15 minutes) and are around a five minute walk from the stadium.

LOCAL RIVALS

Clyde and Albion Rovers.

ADMISSION PRICES

Adults: £8. Concessions: £2.
Parent and Child: £9 (plus £1 per extra child).

PROGRAMME

Official Programme: £1.

RECORD ATTENDANCE

For Hampden:
149,415 - Scotland v England, 1937.
This is the record for the largest attendance at a football match in Britain.
For Queens Park:
95,722 v Rangers (1930).

AVERAGE ATTENDANCE

2003-2004: 516 (Division Three).

OTHER PLACES OF INTEREST

The stadium is also the home of the Scottish Football Museum, which opened its doors in May 2001. I was thoroughly impressed not only with the standard of museum, but also the vast array of items that can be seen, from a ticket from the first ever Football International held in Glasgow in 1872, to an exhibition of football related 'toys'. The current Scottish Cup is also available to view within the museum.

What I particularly liked was the emphasis on the fans' involvement in the Clubs, from the first fanzines to the Tartan Army. The museum is a must see for any true football supporter.

The museum is open daily from 10.00am to 5pm (Sundays 11am-5pm, last admittance all days - 4.15pm). Entrance costs £5 for adults and £2.50 for concessions. Tours of the stadium are also available on non match days for an additional charge of £2.50 adults, £1.25 concessions. If you have an enquiry you can ring the museum on 0141-616-6100. Queens Park offer a joint 'museum entry and match day' ticket for £10.

DID YOU KNOW?

That Queens Park are Scotland's oldest football league club, having been formed in 1867.

RAITH ROVERS

Ground Name: Starks Park
Capacity: 10,104 (all-seated)
Address: Pratt Street, Kirkcaldy KY1 1SA
Telephone No: 01592-263-514
Fax No: 01592-642-833
Pitch Size: 113 x 70 yards
Club Nickname: Rovers
Home Kit Colours: Navy Blue, White & Red
Official Website: www.rrfc.co.uk
Unofficial Websites:
Independent Supporters Trust - www.raithtrust.org.uk
Aberdeen Rover - www.the-aberdeen-rover.20m.com/index.html

WHAT'S THE GROUND LIKE?

The ground has benefited greatly with the redevelopment of both ends. These stands, the North and South, are virtually identical. Both are good sized, single-tiered stands with windshields on either side and unusual floodlights protruding from their roofs. The North Stand is given to away supporters. On one side of the pitch is the Railway Stand, a small, covered, all-seated stand. Opposite must be one of the most unusual Main Stands in Scotland. It is a classic looking old stand that only runs for less than half the length of the pitch, but extends around one corner of the ground. It is a covered seated stand, the seating area of which is raised above pitch level and has a number of supporting pillars. Even so, the stand oozes character, complete with a 'RRFC' gable on its roof. It is just unfortunate that the rest of this side of the ground is empty.

WHAT'S IT LIKE FOR VISITORS?

Away fans are housed in the North Stand at one end of the ground. The angle of the stand is quite steep, ensuring a good view of the playing action. The facilities are also pretty good. If demand requires it, then part of the Railway Stand can also be allocated to the away support.

Andy Turner adds: 'The staff at the ground are welcoming and friendly. The folk who run the supporters' shop, located in the south stand, personify the welcoming nature of the Club as a whole. I recently took a friend, a Plymouth fan, for his first Scottish game and the lads at the shop gave him a commemorative programme as a souvenir. The Chancellor of the Exchequer, Gordon Brown, is to be seen in the little old stand on occasions; apparently he sold programmes in his Kirkcaldy youth and has followed the club all his life'.

WHERE TO DRINK

The most popular bar with away supporters is the Starks Bar, which is right by the ground. Andy Turner adds: 'Raith's support usually congregate at the Novar Bar in Nicol Street. In my opinion though, the best boozer in town is the Harbour Bar. A regular CAMRA award winner whose landlord brews his own excellent ale as well as having wonderfully kept guest beers from around the UK. The pub is on the seafront by the harbour area (hence the name) next to Fife College Priory Campus. It's a fair distance to the ground, but for those who fancy a bracing walk, it's a matter of a hike the length of the seafront. You can still see the floodlights of the "San Starko" in the distance.'

GETTING THERE & WHERE TO PARK

Take the A921 into Kirkcaldy. Turn onto the B9157 (Pratt Street) for the ground, which is well signposted (football traffic) on entering the town. Street parking.

By Train

Kirkcaldy railway station is around a 15 minute walk away from the ground. Leave the station by the exit adjacent to platform two. Walk along Forth Avenue (a large Ford showroom is located there) and up to a small roundabout. Turn right at the roundabout and follow the road, down to the entrance to Beveridge Park and over another roundabout situated there and into Abbotshall Road. This road leads into Pratt Street and to the ground.

LOCAL RIVALS

Dunfermline, Falkirk, and East Fife.

ADMISSION PRICES

Adults: £12. Concessions: £5. Adult + 1 Child: £15.

PROGRAMME

Official Programme: £1.50.

RECORD ATTENDANCE

31,306 v Hearts (1953).

AVERAGE ATTENDANCE

2003-2004: 2,191 (Division One).

DID YOU KNOW?

That the Club named itself after the local Laird (Lord) Raith and the ground was named after its original owner Robert Stark.

ROSS COUNTY

Ground Name: Victoria Park
Capacity: 5,800 (2,800 seated)
Address: Jubilee Road, Dingwall IV15 9QZ
Telephone No: 01349-860-860
Fax No: 01349-866-277
Pitch Size: 100 x 75 yards
Club Nickname: The County
Home Kit Colours: Navy Blue & White
Official Website:
www.rosscountyfootballclub.co.uk
Unofficial Websites:
The Jail Ender - www.geocities.com/thejailender
Ross County Mad (Footy Mad Network) - www.rosscounty-mad.co.uk

WHAT'S THE GROUND LIKE?

Although originally opened in 1929, the ground has a newish feel about it, as significant investment has been put into it in recent years. The West Stand at one side of the pitch is an attractive looking all-seated covered stand, with a row of executive boxes running across the back. Part of this stand is given to away supporters. This stand was originally opened in 1991, but was extended in 2000 so that it now runs for the whole length of the pitch. Opposite is the East Stand, a small, covered, all-seated stand, which was built in 1995. Both ends are similar sized terraces. The home end, the South Terrace (known locally as the Jail End) is covered, whilst the away end, the North Terrace, is uncovered.

WHAT'S IT LIKE FOR VISITORS?

Away fans are primarily housed in the North Terrace at one end of the ground. This area is uncovered, so be prepared to get wet. A better bet may be to head for one of the seats allocated to away supporters in the West Stand at one side of the pitch, as these are covered. Please note though that entrance to the ground is by ticket only, no cash is accepted at the turnstiles. You will need to buy your ticket from the ticket office, which is the dark red portacabin situated by the car park across the road from the West Stand.

WHERE TO DRINK

The ground is a five minute walk from the town centre, where there are plenty of bars to choose from. Scott Armstrong recommends The Mallard as a good friendly pub with excellent bar food. It is located by the railway station and only 300 yards from Victoria Park.

GETTING THERE & WHERE TO PARK

Take the A835 into Dingwall. On approaching the centre, turn right into Park Street and then right onto the High Street. Continue down the High Street and straight on into Ferry Road. The ground is down on the right. If you get lost, follow signs for the railway station, as the ground is right by it. There is a car park at the ground, which costs £2.

By Train

Dingwall train station is only a few minutes walk away from the ground.

LOCAL RIVALS

Inverness Caledonian Thistle.

ADMISSION PRICES

Seating:

Adults: £13. Concessions: £7.

Terrace:

Adults: £11. Concessions: £6.

PROGRAMME

Official Programme: £1.50.

RECORD ATTENDANCE

8,000 v Rangers (1966).

AVERAGE ATTENDANCE

2003-2004: 3,203 (Division One).

DID YOU KNOW?

That with its capacity of 6,000, the ground holds more than the entire population of the town of Dingwall where it is situated.

ST JOHNSTONE

Ground Name: McDiarmid Park
Capacity: 10,673 (all-seated)
Address: Crieff Road, Perth PH1 2SJ
Telephone No: 01738-459-090
Fax No: 01738-625-771
Ticket Office: 01738-455-000
Pitch Size: 115 x 75 yards
Club Nickname: The Saints
Home Kit Colours: Blue & White
Official Website:
www.stjohnstonefc.co.uk
Unofficial Website:
Temple Of Saints - www.grange.demon.co.uk/saints/sjfc.htm

WHAT'S THE GROUND LIKE?

The ground was built in 1989 and replaced the former home of Muirton Park. It consists of four single-tiered stands that are covered and all-seated. Three of the stands are of the same height, with the Main Stand at one side of the ground being a little taller. Overall the ground has a tidy compact feel to it. There is an electric scoreboard situated in one corner of the ground.

WHAT'S IT LIKE FOR VISITORS?

Away fans are normally housed in the North Stand at one end of the ground, where up to 2,000 fans can be accommodated. The facilities in this stand are excellent. The refreshment areas even have TVs above them to keep you amused whilst you are queuing for one of their famous pies. For Old Firm games, the East Stand is also given to away supporters, bringing the total allocation to around 5,000.

WHERE TO DRINK

The closest pub is the 208 Bar which is on Crieff Road about 300 yards away from the ground. The bar is popular with both home and away supporters.

GETTING THERE & WHERE TO PARK

From The South:
Follow the A9 towards Perth and then on reaching Perth continue on the A9 towards Inverness. You will see the ground on your right and at the next roundabout you need

to turn back on yourself and then take the slip road to the ground. The ground is well signposted around the local area.
There is a good sized car park (£2) at the ground, which can take quite some time to exit at the end of a match.

By Train

Perth train station is nearly three miles away from the ground, which is really too far to walk. Get a taxi.

LOCAL RIVALS

Dundee United, Dundee and Falkirk.

ADMISSION PRICES

North Stand:

Adults: £15. Concessions: £5.

PROGRAMME

Official Programme: £1.50.

RECORD ATTENDANCE

10,721 v Rangers, February 26th 1990.

AVERAGE ATTENDANCE

2003-2004: 2,634 (Division One).

DID YOU KNOW?

That the Club derive its name from St.John's Toun (Town), the ancient name for the city of Perth.

ST MIRREN

Ground Name: St Mirren Park (many fans still like to call it Love Street)
Capacity: 10,800 (all-seated)
Address: Love St, Paisley, Renfrewshire PA3 2EJ
Telephone No: 0141-889-2558
Fax No: 0141-848-6444
Ticket Office: 0141-840-4100
Ticket Office Fax: 0141-848-9222
Pitch Size: 110 x 70 yards
Club Nickname: The Buddies
Home Kit Colours: Black & White
Official Website: www.stmirren.net
Unofficial Websites:
Black And White Army - www.blackandwhitearmy.com
St Mirren Info - www.stmirren.info
Independent Supporters Association - www.saintsquarterly.co.uk
St Mirren Mad (Footy Mad Network) - www.stmirren-mad.co.uk

WHAT'S THE GROUND LIKE?

The ground shows both signs of its age and the ambition that is within the Club. The Main Stand is a simple top level and enclosure design stretching only halfway along the pitch straddling the halfway line. This stand is the smallest and oldest of the four. Directly opposite the Main Stand is the North Bank. This holds 4,200 fans and is popular with the hardcore St. Mirren fans. It is a seated terrace with shed style roof stretching the length of the pitch. Access to this stand is by means of a large ramp, which stretches from the North East turnstiles over the corner and into the back of the stand. The Away stand is the Caledonia, or West stand, which is situated at one end of the pitch. This can hold 3,000 away fans but is rarely used completely. The most unusual thing about this stand is that it has a large external staircase on one side, which the away support climbs before embarking down the steeply raked stand. This is because the under croft of the stand is taken up with indoor training pitches. At the other end is the Reid Kerr College Family Stand. This is a 2,200 capacity seated terrace with a cantilevered roof. It was built in order to comply with the Scottish Premier League's rules of having at least 10,000 seats before the club entered the Premier league in 2000.

FUTURE DEVELOPMENTS

David Tennant informs me: 'The Club are hoping to move to a new pupose-built stadium in Greenhill Road, half a mile west of Love Street. Planning permission is expected to be applied for in the near future but the entire project is dependent on the club successfully selling Love St to a supermarket chain'.

WHAT'S IT LIKE FOR VISITORS?

Away fans are normally located in the West section of the North Stand at one side of the pitch. For big games, away fans are given the best seats in the house located in the large Caledonia stand, where up to 3,000 can be accommodated. I have not heard of fans getting hassled outside the ground but caution should be exercised due to its location. The ground can be noisy inside and can on occasions make for an intimidating atmosphere.

WHERE TO DRINK

There are a couple of pubs near the ground, although with the close proximity of the town centre many tend to drink there before heading to the game. The Wee Barrel on Love Street itself is a smallish two-room pub, which gets very busy before games, but on my visit, there was a good mix of home and away support and the service was good. George Clarke adds: 'The Cottage Arms next to a Chinese takeaway just off Greenock Road has long been a popular haunt for away fans, as the away coaches park up near there on Clark Street and it is only a few minutes walk away from the ground'.

GETTING THERE & WHERE TO PARK

Leave the M8 at Junction 29 and take the A726 (Greenock Road) turn towards Paisley town centre. On nearing the town centre you will reach Albion Street and the ground on the left. Street parking.

By Train

Paisley Gilmour Street is on a main line from Glasgow Central Station and is only 400 yards from the ground.

LOCAL RIVALS

Greenock, Morton.

ADMISSION PRICES

North, East and West Stands:

Adults: £12. Concessions: £10. Children: £7.

Parent and Child for North and East Stands:

1 Adult + 1 Child: £16. Each additional child: £4.

Main Stand and Enclosure:

Adults: £13. Concessions: £7.

PROGRAMME

Official Programme: £2.

RECORD ATTENDANCE

47,438 v Celtic, August 20th 1949.

AVERAGE ATTENDANCE

2003-2004: 2,784 (Division One).

DID YOU KNOW?

The Club is named after St Mirren, the Patron Saint of Paisley.

STENHOUSEMUIR

Ground Name: Ochilview Park
Capacity: 5,267 (2,117 seated)
Address: Gladstone Rd, Stenhousemuir FK5 4QL
Telephone No: 01324-562-992
Fax No: 01324-562-980
Pitch Size: 110 x 72 yards
Club Nickname: Warriors
Home Kit Colours: Maroon & White
Official Website:
www.stenhousemuirfc.com
Unofficial Websites:
Norwegian Supporters Club - www.stenhousemuir.com
Stenhousemuir Mad (Footy Mad Network) - www.stenhousemuir-mad.co.uk

WHAT'S THE GROUND LIKE?

After sharing the ground with Falkirk last season, the temporary stands that were built to accommodate the First Division Club have now been removed, so Ochilview is back to how it was a couple of seasons back. On one side of the ground is the relatively new looking Main Stand (also known by the locals as the McCowans End, after the toffee factory in the same street). This small all-seated, covered stand runs for about half the length of the pitch and straddles the halfway line. It has a couple of floodlights perched on its roof. Opposite the stand, the side of the ground not used for spectators houses the team dugouts and a row of small floodlights. A second more substantial sized temporary stand has also been erected at the East end of the ground. At the West end is the medium sized Tryst Road Terrace. This terrace has no roof and on one side there is a Social Club which is owned by the Club. The opposite East End of the ground is again unused by spectators.

FUTURE DEVELOPMENTS

The Club have announced plans to cover the Tryst Road Terrace, with a roof saved from Falkirk's old Brockville Road ground. The works are being funded by a wealthy supporter of the Club. Time scales have yet to be announced as to when this will take place, but it is hoped that it will be completed before the end of the year.

WHAT'S IT LIKE FOR VISITORS?

The ground is largely open having only two sides and generally, there is no segregation of fans for league games. If segregation needs to be enforced, then away fans are predominantly housed in the open terrace which is allocated specifically to them, whilst some seats are also allocated in the Main Stand. If you do end up standing on the open terrace, be prepared to get wet! Please note that once you have gained entrance to the open terrace, transfers to the seated stand are not permitted. Normally a friendly welcome awaits the visiting supporter and I experienced no problems on my visit.

WHERE TO DRINK

There is a Social Club on one corner of the open terrace and a small bar under the Main Stand. Both welcome away supporters, although on occasions the Social Club may charge a small entrance fee for non-members. There are a couple of bars to be found in the nearby town centre (a five minute walk).

GETTING THERE & WHERE TO PARK

Leave the M876 at Junction 2 and follow the A88 towards Stenhousemuir. After about three quarters of a mile turn right into Tryst Road. The ground is down the bottom of this road on the left. It is not the easiest ground to spot as it has no large floodlights that can be seen from a distance. Remember also to ignore the 'football traffic' signs around the area, as if you follow them you will eventually end up at Falkirks' ground. Street parking.

BY TRAIN

The nearest train station is Larbert, which about half a mile away from the ground. As you come out of the station, bear left down the main (King Street) road in front of the station. Continue down this road and you will reach the ground on the left.

LOCAL RIVALS

Falkirk, Stirling Albion and Alloa.

ADMISSION PRICES

Seating:
Adults: £9. Concessions: £5.
Terrace:
Adults: £6. Concessions: £4.

PROGRAMME

Official Programme: £1.20.

RECORD ATTENDANCE

12,500 v East Fife, March 11th 1950 Scottish Cup 4th Round.

AVERAGE ATTENDANCE

2003-2004: 737 (Division Two).

DID YOU KNOW?

The first modern floodlit game in Scotland was played at Ochilview in 1951, when the Club played Hibernian in a friendly.

STIRLING ALBION

Ground Name: Forthbank Stadium
Capacity: 3,808 (2,508 seated)
Address: Springkerse, Stirling FK7 7UJ
Telephone No: 01786-450-399
Fax No: 01786-448-592
Pitch Size: 110 x 74 yards
Club Nickname: Albion or Binos/Beanos
Home Kit Colours: Red & White
Official Website: None at present
Unofficial Websites:
Unofficial Stirling Albion - www.stirlingalbion.com
Red Web - www.stirlingalbionfc.com
Supporters Trust - www.safcst.org.uk

WHAT'S THE GROUND LIKE?

This relatively new ground was opened in 1993, after the Club moved from their original Annfield home. The stadium comprises two seated stands on either side of the pitch and a small terrace at either end. The largest of these stands is the West Stand, which is a covered, single-tier, all-seated stand, that has some executive boxes running across the back of it. Opposite is the similar looking East Stand, which is smaller that the West Stand, not so much in height but in its overall length. This is also covered, all seated and has a Police Control Box situated at its rear. Away fans are allocated this stand. The terraces at each end of the stadium are almost identical. They are small and uncovered box like affairs, which are situated well back from the pitch. These terraces are only opened for the bigger games. Looking out beyond the North Terrace there are some wonderful views of the surrounding countryside. Outside of the stadium there are a number of artificial pitches behind the West Stand.

WHAT'S IT LIKE FOR VISITORS?

Away fans are located in the East Stand at one side of the pitch, where up to 1,000 fans can be seated. This covered stand has good facilities and provides a good view of the playing action. If demand requires it then a further 500 terrace spaces can be provided in the South Terrace.

WHERE TO DRINK

The stadium is on the very outskirts of town, adjacent to a Retail Park, so there is not much around. There is one pub called the Kerse Inn on the Retail Park, which you will pass on your right as you drive down to the stadium.

GETTING THERE & WHERE TO PARK

Leave the M80 at Junction 9 and take the A91 towards Alloa. At the fourth roundabout, turn left and the ground is just down this road on the right. There is a large car park at the ground which is free.

By Train

The stadium is around two miles away from Stirling station, so best jump in a taxi. Otherwise it is a 35-40 minute walk to it.

LOCAL RIVALS

Alloa.

ADMISSION PRICES

Seating:
Adults: £8. Concessions: £5.
Terrace:
Adults: £7. Concessions: £4.

PROGRAMME

Official Programme: £1.

RECORD ATTENDANCE

At Annfield:
26,400 v Glasgow Celtic
Scottish Cup, 4th Round, March 14th 1959.
At Forthbank:
3,808 v Aberdeen
Scottish Cup 4th Round, February 15th, 1996.

AVERAGE ATTENDANCE

2003-2004: 754 (Division Three).

DID YOU KNOW?

The Club previously played at Annfield Park which confused many on a quiz when asked the question, 'Apart from Liverpool, who else plays at a ground called Anfield?'

STRANRAER

Ground Name: Stair Park
Capacity: 5,600 (1,830 seated)
Address: London Road, Stranraer DG9 8BS
Telephone No: 01776-702-194
Fax No: 01776-702-194
Pitch Size: 110 x 70 yards
Club Nickname: The Blues
Home Kit Colours: Royal Blue & White
Official Website: www.stranraerfc.com
Unofficial Websites:
Stranraer Mad (Footy Mad Network) - www.stranraer-mad.co.uk
Stranraerfc.net (Sport Network) - www.stranraerfc.net

WHAT'S THE GROUND LIKE?

The ground is situated in Stair Park, hence the name of the ground. The Club have been playing in the park since 1907, and the park itself even has a bandstand. The ground has seen a lot of improvements in recent years. In 1995 a new Main (South) Stand was constructed at one side of the pitch, built by Barr Construction, at a cost of £500,000. This smart looking covered all-seater stand runs for roughly half the length of the pitch and straddles the half way line. There is a small amount of terracing on each side of the stand. From the back of the Main Stand, you can enjoy good views of the surrounding area to the sea. On the other side is a small stand, that is affectionately known as the 'Coo Shed'. This is a small covered stand that has open terracing on either side of it, as well as a standing area in front. In the rear of this stand are a number of rows of wooden benches. There are also a couple of supporting pillars in this stand. The Town End at one end of the ground is a small covered terrace, whilst at the other end, there is a small open terrace. At the back of this terrace are a number of trees and bushes, which gives the ground a rural look and I noticed a couple of kids seemed to be permanently employed during the game retrieving match balls from the undergrowth (the forwards were not having a good day on my visit!).

WHAT'S IT LIKE FOR VISITORS?

Fans are not normally segregated at Stair Park, but if required then away fans are given the Coo Shed and East Terrace, parts of the ground, where up to 2,000 fans can be accommodated. Away supporters tend to congregate in the Coo Shed as they can make themselves heard better from this stand. The refreshment kiosks offer a selection of scotch pies and sausage rolls at 60p each as well as tea and coffee at 50p per cup. I had an enjoyable afternoon out at Stair Park; however it is worth bearing in mind that when in winter, you should wrap up well as that wind can be biting.

WHERE TO DRINK

There is no club bar at the ground; however it is only a five minute walk from the town centre where there are plenty of bars and eating establishments. As you leave Stair Park, turn left onto the main road to take you down to the town centre. The nearest bar is down on the right, in the Rudicot Hotel. This has a small quiet bar, which has a separate entrance at the side of the hotel. It serves a good pint of real ale (Deuchars IPA). If you continue down into the town centre then the next bar that you come to is 'The Pub' on the left-hand side. This is a fair sized bar with TVs and a pool table. There is a chippy and café on the same side of the road. Colin Ferguson adds: 'Probably the best bet for a drink before the game is the Stranraer FC Social Club which is situated in North Strand Street'.

GETTING THERE & WHERE TO PARK

From The North:
Take the A77 from Glasgow down to Stranraer. This is not a particularly good road, so allow plenty of time for your journey. As you come into Stranraer, either follow the road into the town centre and then turn left onto the A75 (Dumfries) and the ground and park are a short distance down this road on the right. Otherwise turn left from the A77, where the 'football traffic' is indicated by a sign. This takes you up to the A75 and again turn left and the ground and park are over on the right.
From The West:
Follow the A75 into Stranraer. As you pass a school on your right, you will come to the ground and park on your left.

There is free car parking in the park surrounding the ground.
By Train
Stranraer station is a 15 minute walk away from the ground. From the railway station you should walk up to the ferry terminal building, opposite North West Castle Hotel. Turn left, walk about 150 yards to the 'Craig n Elder' Hotel then turn right onto Stair Drive. At the end of Stair Drive turn left. This takes you onto London Road. Walk for about 200 yards and Stair Park is on the right-hand side, actually inside the public park.

Thanks to J McCallum for providing the above directions.

LOCAL RIVALS

Queen Of The South and Ayr United.

ADMISSION PRICES

Main Stand (seating):
Adults: £10. Concessions: £5.
Rest of ground (terrace):
Adults: £8. Concessions: £4.
Children under 12 are admitted free when accompanied by an adult.

PROGRAMME

Official Programme: £1.

RECORD ATTENDANCE

6,500 v Rangers, 1948.

AVERAGE ATTENDANCE

2003-2004: 513 (Division Three).

DID YOU KNOW?

That Stranraer is closer to Belfast in Northern Ireland than it is to Glasgow.

HAMPDEN PARK

Capacity: 52,500 (all-seated)
Address: Letherby Drive, Glasgow, G42 9BA
Scottish Football Association (SFA):
Telephone No: 0141 616 6000
Fax No: 0141 616 6001
Pitch Size: 115 x 75 yards
Year Stadium Opened: 1903
Official Stadium Web Site:
www.hampdenpark.co.uk
SFA Website:
www.scottishfa.co.uk
Scottish Football Museum:
www.scottishfootballmuseum.org.uk/index.html

WHAT'S THE STADIUM LIKE?

Hampden has been completely redeveloped in recent years and the predominantly old terraced ground has now been transformed into a modern all-seated stadium. Although not particularly large for a national stadium, it still retains its charm and individual character, enhanced by its completely enclosed oval shape. Three sides are single tiered, but the South Stand on one side has a small second tier, which slightly overhangs the lower one. Normally this creates an unbalanced look but it has integrated well with the oval stadium roof rising gently towards this stand. There are two electric scoreboards suspended underneath the roofs at each end. One unusual aspect of the stadium is that the team dugouts are actually situated six rows up on the South Stand, allowing team managers to get a better view of the game. The roof of the stadium is adorned with a number of flagpoles and flags, adding to the overall occasion.

With Rangers and Celtic both contesting a number of finals at the stadium, it has now become traditional for each team to be allotted the same ends. So Celtic are allocated the East End and Rangers the West End.

The stadium is also the home of Queens Park FC, who are the only amateur club to compete in the Scottish Football League. The American football team, the Scottish Claymores, are also based at Hampden.

It is occasionally used as a concert venue as well.

WHAT'S IT LIKE FOR VISITORS?

The facilities are pretty good. The concourse is spacious and there is a good selection of food on offer including the 'Hampden Steak Pie' (£1.80), burgers, chips and hot dogs. There are televisions next to the serving areas showing the game being played inside, so that you don't have to miss a kick. There are also Ladbrokes betting facilities available. A tip: if the queues for programmes are quite long outside the stadium, then you can purchase them from programme sellers in the concourse.

Fans are set well back from the playing action as there is quite a gap between the first rows of seats and the pitch. If you are at the back of the ends then this is even more noticeable as you are quite far from the pitch, meaning that you may struggle to see the action at the opposite end. This is not helped by the shallow incline of the stands, which may mean that your view is less than perfect. If possible, it is probably best to obtain tickets in either the North or South Stands, where the views are better. The legroom between rows is good, plus the atmosphere generated within the stadium and the colourful display by the supporters can be superb.

David Tennant, a visiting St Mirren supporter, adds: 'The selection of grub available inside the stadium was impressive. The pies were great and I loved the hamburgers they sold. There are also betting facilities available which is good if you fancy a late wee flutter. The atmosphere generated by the place was, despite its very wide bowl shape, very impressive too'.

WHERE TO DRINK

There are not a great number of bars in the immediate vicinity of the stadium and the few which there are get over-crowded. It is therefore probably best to drink in the City Centre or en route before the game. There are though a number of chippies/kebab shops locally. If you do get there early then my favourite bar in the area is the Clockwork Beer Company on Cathcart Road (going away from the city centre). This spacious pub brews its own varied selection of beers and also stocks a wide range of whiskies - or more affectionately known as the 'water of life'.

GETTING THERE & WHERE TO PARK

Leave the M74 at Junction 1 and turn left at the roundabout into Fullarton Road, following the signs for Rutherglen. Go straight across the next roundabout and at the following roundabout, turn right into Cambuslang Road. You will cross over the River Clyde and then continue to the end of this road. At the traffic lights turn right and continue along Main Street Rutherglen and then on towards Mount Florida. Continue straight along this road until you reach the large Asda Store at which you turn left into Aikenhead Road. The stadium is up this road on the right-hand side.

'It is not straightforward to get to by road and it's not easy to get parked for a big match. So allow plenty of time for your journey' says David Tennant. Parking spaces can typically be found in the area around the Victoria Infirmary.

By Train

The nearest stations to the stadium are Mount Florida and Kings Park. Both are served by trains from Glasgow Central (journey time around 10-15 minutes) and are around a five minute walk away from the stadium.

INTERNATIONAL MATCHES

For International Matches, visiting supporters are housed in the South West corner of the stadium (including a small portion of the upper tier of the South Stand) where around 3,000 supporters can be accommodated. Please note that in common with other Scottish Grounds, alcohol is not available inside the stadium, nor is smoking permitted within the seated areas. The 'Tartan Army of Scottish supporters' are renowned for their friendliness and hospitality, which normally makes for a great visit.

SCOTTISH FOOTBALL MUSEUM

The stadium is also the home of the Scottish Football Museum, which opened its doors in May 2001. I was thoroughly impressed not only with the standard of the museum, but also the vast array of items that can be seen, from a ticket from the first ever Football International held in Glasgow in 1872, to an exhibition of football related 'toys'. The current Scottish Cup is also on view within the museum. What I particularly liked was the emphasis on the fans' involvement in the Clubs, from the first fanzines to the Tartan Army. The museum is a must for any true football supporter.

It is open daily from 10.00am to 5pm (Sundays 11am-5pm, last admittance all days - 4.15pm). Entrance costs: £5 for adults and £2.50 for concessions. If you have an enquiry you can ring the museum on 0141-616-6100. A visit to the museum can also be combined with a tour of the stadium (see below).

STADIUM TOURS

Stadium tours are available each day (except matchdays) for the bargain price of £2.50 adults and £1.25 for concessions, if booked in conjunction with an entrance ticket to the museum. If you just want to book the stadium tour only then this costs £5 for adults and £2.50 for concessions. Family tickets are also available, giving further discounts. The tour lasts about 40 minutes and includes the Presentation Area, Dressing Rooms, Warm Up Area and a walk at pitch side. I found it quite entertaining, interesting and would recommend it. Tours can be booked in advance on 0141-616-6100.

OTHER PLACES OF INTEREST

For all those ground enthusiasts out there, make sure you take a peek at the lesser Hampden, behind the West Stand. This is a small old ground with a quaint looking stand at one side of the pitch. In the past it has been used by Queens Park reserves, as well as for the odd first team outing.

Of equal if not more interest are the remnants of another ground, called Cathkin Park, home to Third Lanark until 1967, when they unfortunately went out of business. The ground was originally built in 1872 and once hosted an international match in 1884, between Scotland and England. There is plenty of terracing still remaining of the old ground, in a picturesque setting and it is only a 10 minute walk away from the present Hampden. The entrance to the park is in Cathcart Road.

RECORD ATTENDANCE

149,415 - Scotland v England, 1937. This is the record for the largest attendance at a football match in Britain.

DID YOU KNOW?

That until 1950, Hampden Park, with a capacity of 150,000, was the world's largest football ground.

ABERDEEN
Ground Name: Pittodrie Stadium
Capacity: 22,199 (all-seated)
Address: Pittodrie Street, Aberdeen, AB24 5QH
Telephone No: 01224-650-400
Fax No: 01224-644-173
Ticket Office: 01224-631-903

AIRDRIE UNITED
Ground Name: Excelsior Stadium (most Airdrie fans still call it New Broomfield)
Capacity: 10,171 (all-seated)
Address: 60 St Enoch Square, Glasgow G1 4AG
Telephone No: 07710-230775
Fax No: 0141-221-1497

ALBION ROVERS
Ground Name: Cliftonhill Stadium
Capacity: 2,496 (489 seated)
Address: Main St, Coatbridge, Lanarkshire ML5 3RB
Telephone No: 01236-606-334
Fax No: 01236-606-334

ALLOA ATHLETIC
Ground Name: Recreation Park
Capacity: 3,100 (400 seated)
Address: Clackmannan Rd, Alloa, FK10 1RY
Telephone No: 01259-722-695
Fax No: 01259-210-886

ARBROATH
Ground Name: Gayfield Park
Capacity: 6,488 (714 seated)
Address: Arbroath, Angus, DD11 1QB
Telephone No: 01241-872-157
Fax No: 01241-431-125

AYR UNITED
Ground Name: Somerset Park
Capacity: 10,243 (1,549 seated)
Address: Tryfield Place, Ayr KA8 9NB
Telephone No: 01292-263-435
Fax No: 01292-281-314

BERWICK RANGERS
Ground Name: Shielfield Park
Capacity: 4,131 (1,366 seated)
Address: Tweedmouth, Berwick-upon-Tweed TD15 2EF
Telephone No: 01289-307-424
Fax No: 01289-307-424

BRECHIN CITY
Ground Name: Glebe Park
Capacity: 3,960 (seated 1,519)
Address: Trinity Rd, Brechin, Angus DD9 6BJ
Telephone No: 01356-622-856
Fax No: 01356-625524

CELTIC
Ground Name: Celtic Park
Capacity: 60,832 (all-seated)
Address: 18 Kerrydale St, Glasgow G40 3RE
Telephone No: 0141-556-2611
Fax No: 0141-551-8106

CLYDE
Ground Name: Broadwood Stadium
Capacity: 8,029 (all-seated)
Address: Ardgoil Drive Cumbernauld G68 9NE
Telephone No: 01236-451-511
Fax No: 01236-733-490

COWDENBEATH
Ground Name: Central Park
Capacity: 5,268 (1,622 seated)
Address: Cowdenbeath, Fife KY4 9QQ
Telephone No: 01383-610-166
Fax No: 01383-512-132

DUMBARTON
Ground Name: Strathclyde Homes Stadium
Capacity: 2,050 (all-seated)
Address: Castle Road, Dumbarton G82 1JJ
Telephone No: 01389-762-569
Fax No: 01389-762-629

DUNDEE
Ground Name: Dens Park
Capacity: 12,085 (all-seated)
Address: Sandeman St, Dundee DD3 7JY
Telephone No: 01382-889-966
Fax No: 01382-832-284

DUNDEE UNITED
Ground Name: Tannadice Park
Capacity: 14,209 (all-seated)
Address: Tannadice St, Dundee DD3 7JW
Telephone No: 01382-833-166
Fax No: 01382-889-398

DUNFERMLINE
Ground Name: East End Park
Capacity: 11,998 (all-seated)
Address: Halbeath Rd, Dunfermline, Fife KY12 7RB
Telephone No: 01383-724-295
Fax No: 01383-723-468
Ticket Office No: 0870-300-1201
Ticket Office Fax: 01383-626-452

EAST FIFE
Ground Name: Bayview Stadium
Capacity: 2,000 (all-seated)
Address: Harbour View, Methil, Fife KY8 3RW

Telephone No: 01333-426-323
Fax No: 01333-426-376

EAST STIRLINGSHIRE
Ground Name: Firs Park
Capacity: 1,880 (200 seated)
Address: Firs Street, Falkirk FK2 7AY
Telephone No: 01324 623-583
Fax No: 01324 637-862

ELGIN CITY
Ground Name: Borough Briggs
Capacity: 3,927 (478 seated)
Address: Borough Briggs Road, Elgin IV30 1AP
Telephone No: 01343-551-114
Fax No: 01343-547-921

FALKIRK
Ground Name: Falkirk Stadium
Capacity: 4,200 (all-seated)
Address: Westfield, Falkirk FK2 9DX
Telephone No: 01324-666-808
Fax No: 01324-664-539

FORFAR ATHLETIC
Ground Name: Station Park
Capacity: 4,602 (seated 739)
Address: Carseview Road, Forfar, Angus DD8 3BT
Telephone No: 01307-463-576
Fax No: 01307-466-956

GRETNA
Ground Name: Raydale Park
Capacity: 2,200
Address: Dominion Road, Gretna DG16 5AP
Telephone No: 01461-337-602
Fax No: 01461-338-047

HAMILTON ACADEMICAL
Ground Name: New Douglas Park
Capacity: 5,300 (all-seated)
Address: Cadzow Avenue, Hamilton, Lanarkshire ML3 0FT
Telephone No: 01698-383-650
Fax No: 01698-285-422

HAMPDEN PARK
Capacity: 52,500 (all-seated)
Address: Letherby Drive, Glasgow, G42 9BA
Scottish Football Association (SFA):
Telephone No: 0141 616 6000
Fax No: 0141 616 6001

HEART OF MIDLOTHIAN
Ground Name: Tynecastle Stadium
Capacity: 18,008 (all-seated)
Address: Gorgie Rd, Edinburgh EH11 2NL
Telephone No: 0131-200-7200
Fax No: 0131-200-7222

HIBERNIAN
Ground Name: Easter Road
Capacity: 17,500 (all-seated)
Address: 12 Albion Place, Edinburgh EH7 5QG
Telephone No: 0131-661-2159
Fax No: 0131-659-6488
Ticket Office: 0131-661-1875

INVERNESS CALEDONIAN THISTLE
Ground Name: Caledonian Stadium
Capacity: 6,500 (2,200 seated)
Address: East Longman, Inverness IV1 1FF
Telephone No: 01463-222-880
Fax No: 01463-715-816

KILMARNOCK
Ground Name: Rugby Park
Capacity: 18,128 (all-seated)
Address: Rugby Park, Kilmarnock KA1 2DP
Telephone No: 01563-545-300
Fax No: 01563-522-181

LIVINGSTON
Ground Name: City Stadium (still known to many fans as Almondvale)
Capacity: 10,000 (all-seated)
Address: Livingston, West Lothian EH54 7DN
Telephone No: 01506-417-000
Fax No: 01506-418-888

MONTROSE
Ground Name: Links Park
Capacity: 3,292 (1,338 seated)
Address: Wellington St, Montrose DD10 8QD
Telephone No: 01674-673-200
Fax No: 01674-677-311

MORTON
Ground Name: Cappielow Park
Capacity: 11,100 (seated 5,741)
Address: Sinclair Street, Greenock PA15 2TY
Telephone No: 01475 723-571
Fax No: 01475 781-084

MOTHERWELL
Ground Name: Fir Park
Capacity: 13,742 (all-seated)
Address: Fir Park, Motherwell ML1 2QN
Telephone No: 01698-333-333
Fax No: 01698-276-333

PARTICK THISTLE
Ground Name: Firhill Stadium
Capacity: 13,079 (10,887 seated)
Address: 80 Firhill Road, Glasgow G20 7AL
Telephone No: 0141-579-1971
Fax No: 0141-945-1525

PETERHEAD

Ground Name: Balmoor Stadium
Capacity: 4,000 (998 seated)
Address: Lord Catto Park, Peterhead AB42 1EU
Telephone No: 01779-478-256
Fax No: 01779-490-682

QUEEN OF THE SOUTH

Ground Name: Palmerston Park
Capacity: 6,412 (3,509 seated)
Address: Dumfries, DG2 9BA
Telephone No: 01387-254-853
Fax No: 01387-240-470

QUEENS PARK

Ground Name: Hampden Park
Capacity: 52,500 (all-seated)
Address: Mount Florida, Glasgow G42 9BA
Telephone No: 0141-632-1275
Fax No: 0141-636-1612

RAITH ROVERS

Ground Name: Starks Park
Capacity: 10,104 (all-seated)
Address: Pratt Street, Kirkcaldy KY1 1SA
Telephone No: 01592-263-514
Fax No: 01592-642-833

RANGERS

Ground Name: Ibrox Stadium
Capacity: 50,411 (all-seated)
Address: 150 Edmiston Drive, Glasgow, G51 2XD
Telephone No: 0870-600-1972
Fax No: 0870-600-1978

ROSS COUNTY

Ground Name: Victoria Park
Capacity: 5,800 (2,800 seated)
Address: Jubilee Road, Dingwall IV15 9QZ
Telephone No: 01349-860-860
Fax No: 01349-866-277

ST MIRREN

Ground Name: St Mirren Park (many fans still like to call it Love Street)
Capacity: 10,800 (all-seated)
Address: Love St, Paisley, Renfrewshire PA3 2EJ
Telephone No: 0141-889-2558
Fax No: 0141-848-6444
Ticket Office: 0141-840-4100
Ticket Office Fax: 0141-848-9222

STENHOUSEMUIR

Ground Name: Ochilview Park
Capacity: 5,267 (2,117 seated)
Address: Gladstone Rd, Stenhousemuir FK5 4QL
Telephone No: 01324-562-992
Fax No: 01324-562-980

STIRLING ALBION

Ground Name: Forthbank Stadium
Capacity: 3,808 (2,508 seated)
Address: Springkerse, Stirling FK7 7UJ
Telephone No: 01786-450-399
Fax No: 01786-448-592

ST JOHNSTONE

Ground Name: McDiarmid Park
Capacity: 10,673 (all-seated)
Address: Crieff Road, Perth PH1 2SJ
Telephone No: 01738-459-090
Fax No: 01738-625-771

STANRAER

Ground Name: Stair Park
Capacity: 5,600 (1,830 seated)
Address: London Road, Stranraer DG9 8BS
Telephone No: 01776-702-194
Fax No: 01776-702-194